Investors in People
in the Church

GS Misc 545

Investors in People in the Church

The introduction of the Investors Standard in dioceses, parishes and cathedrals

**Report of a Board of Education Task Group
by Julian Cummins and Ian Stubbs**

CHURCH HOUSE
PUBLISHING

Church House Publishing
Church House
Great Smith Street
London
SW1P 3NZ

ISBN 0 7151 4922 9

Published 1999 for the Board of Education of the Church of England by
Church House Publishing

This report has only the authority of the working group which produced it. It has been
approved by the Board of Education.

Printed by The Cromwell Press Ltd, Trowbridge, Wiltshire

Contents

7.   Conclusions   **77**

Preface

I am pleased to commend this Report to the Church of England. Investors in People is a standard of excellence in organizations of every kind. It is now being seen nationally as the general standard in both public and private sectors and used by both large and small organizations. At the heart of Investors are four important and fundamental principles – sense of purpose, the contribution everyone can make, the training and support people need, the identification of what is being achieved.

In many ways this is common sense and what good organizations are doing all the time. But we know from experience that whilst there is much to celebrate in the Church at all levels, much also remains to be done. The report comments, for example, on the need to develop clearer and more realistic and achievable aims, better coordination, improved communication as well as learning from our best practice and our mistakes through more effective evaluation of all that we undertake. With the growing significance throughout the church of collaborative ministry there is also the need to improve the support and training of everyone involved in the churchís mission and ministry, at every level. We need to consider how our life and work together can be deepened and made more effective in the kind of world we are moving into. There is much to be gained from making use of a common framework such as Investors.

Some people may be concerned that this is merely another sign of the Church being taken over by inappropriate secular management theories and practices. They will question whether there are more spiritual ways of developing our corporate life. The Report carefully considers the theological significance of Investors and concludes that, though imperfect as all human structures are, it embodies values which are congruent with those of the Gospel – that people matter, that everyone should be involved and supported, the stewardship and efficient use of God-given resources, the vital interplay between the local and the catholic. Some of the language used by Investors may seem unfamiliar or out of place in a church setting but the Report also shows how it can be translated. Experience shows that Investors can help the Church to clarify its mission, foster the gifts within the body of Christ, help people grow in the Spirit and enable us to reflect theologically.

I am aware from my own experience that Investors is demanding. It takes commitment, time and resources. But nothing less is required if we are, in obedience to God's mission in the contemporary world, to become a learning church and grow as disciples of Christ.

✠ David Ripon
Chairman, Board of Education of the Church of England

Foreword

What unites all organizations, public, private or voluntary is the fact that we can only move forward if we understand where we are trying to go and what we need to do to get there.

Fundamental to the Investors in People Standard is the need for organizations to set themselves clear goals and work with all their people to find the best way of achieving them. This, as the seven million people who are working with the Standard in the UK have found, is no more than common sense. But it is in the nature of the busy, complicated and sometimes frustrating world that we live in, that common sense is not always commonly found.

Investors in People provides a framework which has been proven to make organizations of all types successful, by ensuring that the way ahead is properly thought ahead and that everyone has the awareness and the ability to make their contribution. Whatever end the organization is seeking to reach, Investor in People is the effective means.

In an environment such as the Church, where the people concerned come from many different backgrounds and have a hugely diverse range of knowledge and skills, this proposition must be a very exciting one. I commend the Standard to you and hope that it will play an important role in bringing everyone's contribution together.

Ruth Spellman
Chief Executive, Investors in People UK

Introduction

In the last few years some Anglican dioceses and parishes have been using, and others are planning to use, Investors in People. Investors, as it is commonly called, is a standard of excellence for organizations of every kind. It is one of the most widely recognized tools for planning, development and training. Schools, voluntary groups, charities, political parties, hospitals and so forth are working towards it, as are companies in the private sector.

By the end of 1998 there were 11,300 recognized Investors in People organizations, and a total of 32,600 were formally committed to the Standard. This means that over 3 million employees are involved, representing over one third of employed people in Britain. Of the recognized organizations, 4,000 have fewer than 50 employees. *The Learning Age: A Renaissance for a New Britain*, the Government's Green Paper on Lifelong Learning published by the DfEE in February 1998, states a commitment to consolidate the position of Investors in People as the general standard across the public and private sectors, and in large and small organizations. Also, the aim is that every Government department should be an Investor in People by the year 2000.

Terms of reference

Following the introduction of Investors in the Diocese of Ripon, it was suggested that experience here and in other parts of the Church should be used to see if the Standard could be commended to other dioceses as a helpful tool for mission and ministry. The Board of Education Investors in People Task Group was set up in 1997 (membership in Appendix 1) in order to: examine how dioceses and parishes are making use of Investors; examine the theological implications; and make recommendations as to the Standard's further application.

The Task Group was given the following terms of reference:

1. to evaluate the experience of Investors in the Church of England and in the other mainstream Christian denominations;

2. to establish guidelines in association with Investors in People UK for the interpretation and application of the Investors Standard in the Church of England;

3. to articulate and recommend a clear theological rationale for Investors;

4. to recommend means of implementing Investors which take account of the specific mission, structure and organization of the Church of England, together with its cultural and theological diversity;

5. to initiate the development of materials, training and support systems for the implementation of Investors in the Church;

6. to share experience with ecumenical partners and with those parts of the Anglican Communion where Investors is established;

7. to make recommendations regarding provision for the continuing support and resourcing of Investors in the Church.

The Learning Age

This report is written at a time when, in our national life and in the life of the Church, growing importance is being attached to lifelong learning. In *The Learning Age*, David Blunkett, the Secretary of State for Education, describes a vision of lifelong learning:

> As well as securing our economic future, learning has a wider contribution. It helps make ours a civilised society, develops the spiritual side of our lives and promotes active citizenship. Learning enables people to play a full part in their community. It strengthens the family, the neighbourhood and consequently the nation. It helps us to fulfil our potential and opens doors to a love of music, art and literature. That is why we value learning for its own sake as well as for the equality of opportunity it brings. Learning is essential to the development of fulfilled and productive human beings. (DfEE, 1998)

In the same way, the bishops at the 1998 Lambeth Conference linked learning, mission and ministry in one of the resolutions of the Conference. This said that all members, in order to realize their sharing in the common priesthood of the Church, 'should be given education and opportunity for ministries which include worship, witness, service and acts of forgiveness and reconciliation in the setting of their daily life'(Lambeth Conference, 1998. Res.111.22). It is appropriate, therefore, that this report will be presented to the General Synod in July 1999, at the same time as the report of the Board's Working Party on Lay Discipleship.

But learning is not only an activity of the individual and is more than the offering of opportunities. *The Learning Age* stresses the development of a learning culture, at the core of which is the notion of a society continuously learning and adapting to new circumstances. Similarly, the idea of the learning organization contains the twin notions of direction or purpose and continuous learning. In setting up the Investors in People Task Group, the Board of Education felt that it was the emphasis of Investors on the development of the learning organization that had something important to offer the Church as it seeks to adapt to the changing circumstances and challenges of a new millennium. This is very much in line with the thinking in *Working As One Body*, the Report of the Archbishops' Commission on the Organization of the Church of England (the Turnbull Report). The report sees a concealed presupposition in the four classic marks of the life of the Church – one, holy, catholic and apostolic – that it must be a learning community. This emphasis gained further endorsement at the July 1998 Synod in York, when Professor David Ford, in a Bible Exposition on Ephesians, ventured that:

> If I were choosing one overarching commitment which it would be wise for a Church such as ours to make in a culture such as ours it would be one which occurs at several points in the Turnbull Report: to be a learning church. (Ford, 1998)

Learning is fundamental to the faithfulness and effectiveness of a Church seeking to proclaim the gospel afresh to each generation and context. The development of a learning Church could be described in terms of attention to a set of key tasks summarized as:

1. the fostering of corporate spirituality which values creativity, learning and collaboration;

2. the translation of the Church's ongoing mission into shared practical, achievable and flexible targets and steps;

3. the fostering of connections between the catholic and the local, the whole and the parts;

4. enabling people to identify gifts and skills and take up their role;

5. the provision of support and training for understanding and growth, as well as technical skills;

6. a continuing cycle of evaluation, learning from experience and revision of plans.

The purpose of this report is to describe the Investors process in detail and to spell out in practical terms how it has been applied in several different contexts in the Church. We also offer the report as a handbook to dioceses, deaneries, parishes and cathedrals that wish to work towards the

Investors in People Standard. Chapter 6, in particular, is in the form of more practical questions and guidelines.

The scope of the report

This report is addressed to the Church of England. Investors in People operates on slightly different boundaries, embracing England, Wales, Scotland and Northern Ireland but with special arrangements for the Channel Islands, the Isle of Man and parts of mainland Europe.

We are aware of the debate about the role of 'management' and the use of management techniques in the Church. Some see the adoption of such techniques as an uncritical appropriation of the secular spirit of the age when what is required is attention to the fundamentals of faith. The Task Group has gone to considerable lengths to reflect theologically on the general issues of management as well as on particular questions arising from Investors in People. We believe that there are important theological questions to be addressed, that these can be answered and that it is important to distinguish between theological validity on the one hand and stubborn resistance to change on the other, sometimes veiled in theological language!

The members of the Task Group met eight times. We made visits to the Dioceses of Ripon, Bath and Wells, Bangor and Blackburn, to Lichfield Cathedral and to the parish of St Barnabas, Lenton Abbey. The Group has conducted a questionnaire survey of parishes in Ripon Diocese and of General Synod members, and has written to all diocesan secretaries. The work of the Group has mainly centred on experience in Anglican churches. We have spoken to ecumenical colleagues through the auspices of CCBI and CTE but it seems that, to date, experience in other denominations is limited.

We have also drawn on the expertise of a Technical Group of Investors practitioners. They include some of the most senior and experienced practitioners in the country. The members of this group, listed in Appendix 2, are all active church members, including one Roman Catholic member. They include Investors advisers and assessors and consultants with experience of this and other quality-management approaches. All the members of the Technical Group have experience of the application of Investors in charities, schools and voluntary-sector organizations, as well as in commercial and industrial sectors. The work done by the Technical Group reinforces our view that the expertise of lay people, together with their willingness to make it available to the Church, is one of the Church's major but under-utilized resources.

We are particularly grateful to Julian Cummins, whose expertise in this field has been invaluable. He undertook many of the visits and wrote this report, together with Ian Stubbs. Thanks are also due to David MacPherson, who carried out the survey of Ripon Diocese; lay people in the parish of St Barnabas, Lenton Abbey; Professor Haddon Willmer, who acted as a theological consultant; Mary Sinker, who read and commented on some initial drafts of the report; and many people from Investors and from dioceses who gave us help and information.

1

The Investors Standard

When people talk about Investors in People ('Investors' for short) they can mean a number of different things. They can mean the words of the Standard itself – 23 'indicators' tersely expressed in just 400 words (see Appendix 4). They can mean the principles that lie behind the words, of which the indicators are no more than 'indicative'. They can mean a particular Investors project experienced at work, which may have been well run, or sometimes perhaps was badly run. Or they can mean the sum of these things – the Standard, the principles behind it, and the immensely varied experiences people have had of putting Investors into practice in more than 30,000 organizations. This chapter takes a comprehensive look at what Investors is and how it works, starting with its origins and purpose. Some experiences of Investors have been negative, and that evidence is as important as positive experiences. A balanced assessment requires a careful analysis of the range of experience, and of its relation to the principles, wording, purpose and operation of the Standard.

Origins and purpose

During the 1980s, concern grew about the level of training and development in UK workplaces. By international comparisons, standards were poor. Traditional apprenticeships had collapsed, and had not been replaced by new mechanisms. The key to success in every kind of organization was increasingly seen to lie in a well-trained and well-motivated workforce. Surveys suggested that employers acknowledged the importance of training, but that their performance lagged behind their words.

Unions, government and companies together formulated a series of initiatives to address the training challenge in the late 1980s. Training and Enterprise Councils (TECs) were created across the country to spearhead skill development. The National Council for Vocational Qualifications (NCVQ) was formed to build a new framework of qualifications based on competence (i.e. knowledge, skills and aptitudes required to fulfil a particular task) rather than solely on book knowledge. National Training Awards were introduced to celebrate best practice in training and development.

Investors in People was conceived in 1989, in parallel with these other initiatives. The initial suggestion was that it be called 'Investors in Training'. Its concept was very simple: to summarize good practice in training and development; to express that as a series of principles and indicators; to enable organizations to demonstrate that they met that good practice; and to help them continually improve. Investors was thus part of a multi-pronged and broadly based strategy to meet Britain's training challenge.

Following a series of trials, Investors was formally launched in October 1991. All these initiatives are still with us, and the passage of time has reinforced their importance. The present Government's Green Paper *The Learning Age: a Renaissance for a New Britain* (DFEE, 1998) builds on and extends them. Nationally, the scoreboard is mixed. By the end of 1997, 14 million people had achieved NVQ level 2 (equivalent to five higher-grade GCSEs), and the proportion of graduates in the working population had doubled over the previous decade. But one in five adults had poor literacy and numeracy skills, and at NVQ level 3 (the equivalent of two A levels) Britain still lagged behind France, Germany, the USA and Singapore.

Employers are not the only focus of *The Learning Age*, but they are a key part of the picture. In practice, the workplace is a major focus for lifelong learning. The Green Paper gives pride of place to Investors as the standard for training and development in organizations and as the most widely recognized tool for organizations to use in planning the current and future development of their staff to meet business aims. Investors has a clear link with improved business performance:

> We propose to consolidate the position of Investors in People as the general Standard across the public and private sectors, and in large and small organizations. (DFEE, 1998)

A business or general standard?

The Government has said that every Government department should be an Investor by the year 2000. It also talks about 'business aims' and 'business performance' when discussing Investors. Is Investors for business? Or is it for everyone? In which case, why does it use business language?

One member of our Task Group worked on early drafts of the Standard. He recalls that the major challenge was to convince business leaders to take training seriously: 'We had to use language that cut ice with chief executives.' This resulted in the strongly 'business-focused' language of the Standard. At first, the language proved a major problem in non-profit organizations. But, in practice, several thousand schools, hospitals, local

2

authorities and other public and voluntary organizations have overcome the problem. They have interpreted 'business' to mean 'organizational' and understood other language in the Standard in a similar way. There is a strategic review of the Standard taking place in 1999 and part of the Task Group's submission is reproduced in Appendix 5. There are two strategies for the Church:

- to develop a glossary to interpret the language of the Standard. This approach is shown in Appendix 3;

- to transliterate Investors terminology into the equally technical language of the Church. This is shown in Appendix 4.

Whichever strategy is adopted, it is important to see that Investors is a common standard applicable to all organizations. Its language has to be interpreted for each context. This applies as much to very different kinds of business organization as it does to the infinite variety of non-profit organizations. It also applies in Wales, where the translation of the Standard into Welsh is subject to all the ambiguities with which Bible translators are familiar. Indeed, some could argue that the word 'Investor' is primarily associated with money and profit, and only secondarily with the use of time and effort to make something a success. The Welsh 'Busoddwyr' particularly carries the notion of financial risk. The Task Group considered using different language. It concluded that to do so would evade the Church's responsibility to engage constructively in contemporary society and in the language used by that society. For this reason we have retained Investors in the title of this report.

Do you do, use or meet Investors?

The choice of verb for engaging with Investors says a great deal about your understanding of its relationship to an organization and its purpose:

- *Doing* Investors implies that it is separate from normal activities. ('I'm not doing any pastoral work today. I'm too busy doing Investors.')

- *Using* Investors implies that it is a self-sufficient tool that can help what you are doing. ('I'm using Investors to re-jig our pastoral programme.')

- *Meeting* the Investors Standard implies that it is a benchmark rather than a tool, and you supply the content. ('I think our pastoral team now meets the Standard.')

3

'Doing' Investors is almost always a mistake. A Standard of just 400 words is difficult to 'use' without further elaboration. What organizations 'do' is to be a school, business or church. They 'use' wide ranges of tools. Investors in People is just one of the tools available for them to use. They can judge their progress by the extent to which they 'meet' the Standard – but that is never an end in itself.

Can you 'meet' the Standard without ever consciously 'doing' Investors? Of course, and the reverse is also true. 'Using Investors' means that the focus is kept on the organization and its purpose.

Just how different is Investors?

There are two dangers in talking about Investors. One is to say how different it is (which devalues things people are doing already). The other is to say that it isn't different at all (in which case, why bother with it?). The truth is that it is similar to well-respected models widely used in the Church, and builds on them.

Those who have used parish audit and planning will immediately recognize processes for discerning purpose, developing plans and evaluating them, but will find that the emphasis on training and its integration into purpose and plans gives an added dimension. Those familiar with the Pastoral Cycle will recognize the cycle of purpose, planning, action and evaluation as a model extensively used in spiritual and pastoral work and will find that its application to church life makes eminent sense. Those who work in lay training and with ministerial review will recognize large elements of the Standard that deal with training and development, and will find its integration into planning a logical next step. That this should be so is not surprising. Investors is a summary of good practice, and there is plenty of good practice to be found in the Church.

Why external standards?

Some people question why the Church should even think about external standards. The reality is that they are part of modern life. New rules about annual reports and accounts, health and safety legislation, child protection procedure . . . the list is endless. Many standards are obligatory, but many are voluntary – such as external validation in most ministerial training. The question is not 'Should we use external standards?' – we do so extensively – but 'Which external standards will most help us be the Body of Christ?' Investors needs to be judged on that criterion.

4

The content of the Investors Standard

The Investors Standard is printed at Appendix 4. It does not take long to read, but it is difficult to understand at first reading. This is not accidental. The Standard is a summary of good practice, a set of indicators, a benchmark of performance, a framework for development. It makes very little sense when separated from its principles and application. So how do those new to it best approach it? At courses about Investors, participants in small groups of two or three are asked to apply the Standard to their own organizations. To make sense of it, readers should stop reading and start applying. There are three ways to do so, all of them practical. They can be undertaken alone, but are best done with one or two others.

1 Apply the indicators to your local church

Start with Indicator 1.1: 'The commitment from top management to train and develop employees is communicated effectively throughout the organization.' Is that true in your parish? How is such commitment expressed? Do PCC members, for example, feel that the parish is committed to their development? Is it shown in induction courses for new PCC members? Was the treasurer offered training in the new charity legislation?

Then take Indicator 1.2: 'Employees at all levels are aware of the broad aims or vision of the organization.' 'Employees' means anyone for whose training the organization is responsible – so, in the local church, that means the PCC, anyone leading a group, and anyone with a defined function. Are they all aware of the broad aims or vision of the parish? Could they express it in their own words?

As you go through the indicators, you'll find some that your parish already meets and others that it doesn't. That's not surprising: a summary of best practice means that most of us have achieved some of it, and some of us a great deal of it. Many organizations find that the last few indicators – about evaluation – are their weak point. Others find they grind to a halt at Indicator 2.1 – they simply don't have a plan of what they are trying to do. Very few can say, hand on heart, that they meet every indicator.

Looked at in this way, the Standard is a mirror of your parish's approach to planning, training and evaluation.

2 Apply the 'acid test'

Greater Nottingham TEC in whose area St Barnabas, Lenton Abbey is situated, found a shorter way to see if an organization broadly met the

Standard. This 'acid test' uses more neutral language than the Standard. In a church setting, you can interpret 'manager' as anyone, lay or ordained, who carries oversight for particular work, and 'job' as a role or task that people take on.

> We are an Investor in People if the majority of people in our organization can:
>
> - explain the organization's objectives and goals;
>
> - explain the importance of their job in relationship to the organization's success;
>
> - demonstrate how training and development have helped them improve their contribution to the organization;
>
> - tell you that their manager is competent and committed to coaching and developing them;
>
> - accept responsibility to improve themselves and their job continuously.

The best way to use this is to ask people! Take stewards and welcomers ('sidespeople'), for example. Can they explain the parish's objectives and goals, and explain the importance of their job in relation to those objectives and goals? Can they demonstrate that they have been trained and developed to improve the way they do their job, and that whoever is responsible for the rota is committed, as they are, to improving their ministry of welcome? If you think of the importance that first contact has for newcomers to a church, these are practical and important questions. Then try out the 'acid test'on group leaders, PCC members, the worship group and others. It will soon become clear what Investors is about.

3 Look at the principles in practice

The Investors indicators fall into four principles: commitment, planning, action and evaluation. These can be expressed as a cycle, as below. The cycle is common sense – but it is not always easy to apply. To see how it works, take a project in the recent life of your parish: for example, the introduction of an Alpha or Emmaus group, or the introduction of a new form of all-age worship. Ask yourself the following questions.

> COMMITMENT. Was it clear to all those involved that they would be trained for their role? Did they understand what they were doing and why?

PLANNING. Did you have a plan for the project? Did it specify who needed training and the resources needed? Did it link to the overall parish plan?

ACTION. Did the training take place? What did it consist of? Were the people who gave the training competent?

EVALUATION. Was the project successful? What lessons were learnt? Did training make any difference? Did the project contribute to the parish aims and vision?

Of course, no-one is perfect. The idea of a cycle is that it encourages continuous improvement. If you identified any shortcomings, how would you do better next time?

Thinking about the Investors indicators in this way will turn them from a dry set of words into the basis of an analysis of how your parish really works, and how it could do better. Remember, Investors did not start with theory, but with observed best practice. The indicators are a distillation of good practice. They come alive only when they are applied.

The operation of Investors

There is nothing to stop any organization equipped with a copy of the Investors Standard from checking how it stands against it, improving as appropriate, and leaving it there. But, in practice, organizations need help in this process, and often want recognition of their achievement. There is a national structure to provide that help and recognition.

Investors in People UK (IIPUK) has responsibility for protecting and interpreting the Standard; validating training courses for advisers and assessors; and ensuring that the Standard is understood and applied consistently. IIPUK also licenses the Standard for use elsewhere, for example in Australia, parts of Europe and the Isle of Man.

Training and Enterprise Councils (TECs) are responsible for promoting the Standard locally. The Government has given them targets as part of its 'learning age strategy'. TECs mostly employ advisers, or authorize consultants as advisers, who often run training courses and can give support to organizations wanting to apply Investors.

Assessors are called in when an organization wants recognition as an Investor in People. Assessors are moderated by national quality arrangements to ensure a consistency of assessment across the country.

There are typically six steps in engaging with Investors. Organizations drop out of this six-stage process at various points. The action plan may never be drawn up, or implementation may falter. Some feel that external recognition is not necessary, and some fail to achieve it. Others obtain their plaque, and then lose interest. Negative experiences of Investors are often associated with organizations that have not pursued the process right the way through.

Six steps for engaging with Investors

1. IS IT FOR US?

Doing Investors must contribute to an organization's purpose. It must make it a better firm, a better school or a better church. So, having read about the Standard, the first question to ask is 'Is it for us?' If you cannot see the benefit, it is not worth proceeding.

2. A DIAGNOSTIC EXERCISE

At step 1, you will have made an initial assessment of where you stand in relation to the Standard. The second step is to make a more structured analysis of the indicators you meet, the indicators you nearly meet, and the indicators which you miss by a mile. This requires a careful diagnosis of the organization, and particularly its planning, training and evaluation processes.

3. AN ACTION PLAN

This is the plan of action to enable you to meet the Standard. Sometimes it is a plan just for Investors. More often, it forms part of a wider plan. In schools, it can be part of the School Development Plan. In parishes, it can be part of an existing plan for mission and nurture. In every situation, the action plan will start with existing good practice, and build on existing plans and programmes.

4. IMPLEMENTATION OF THE ACTION PLAN

This stage can last for as little as a year or as long as five years or more. Many organizations start with over-ambitious timetables. It is better to aim for steady progress, consistent with other aims and needs. Sometimes, implementation is carried out under an Investors label. More and more, organizations use labels that reflect their own culture and priorities.

5. ASSESSMENT AND RECOGNITION

Most organizations, when they feel they meet the Standard, apply for external assessment for recognition as Investors. This entitles them to use the Investors plaque and logo. The real value of recognition is that it represents an impartial external view of progress made and improvements that are still continuing.

6. CONTINUOUS IMPROVEMENT

Investors does not end with first recognition. People, needs and organizations change. There are always things that can be done better. Recognition lasts for three years. The option of a rolling annual re-assessment has recently been introduced, and most organizations are now taking this. Those recognized early on are now on their third triennial recognition. Many feel that it is only the second time round that they really understand what Investors is about, and gain the full benefits.

The benefits of Investors

Does Investors make a difference? The Institute of Employment Studies (IES) surveyed 1,800 firms over a period of three years. Their sample was balanced between sizes and types of firm, and covered those recognized as Investors through to those with no involvement at all. They concluded:

> It is clear from these results that organizations involved in Investors adopted a materially different approach to the management of their training to those who were not. (Hillage and Moralee, 1996)

Also, respondents in the survey believed that Investors provided an impetus to bring about changes: 74 per cent of those organizations involved in Investors identified improved training systems as a key benefit, and only 15 per cent thought they would have made the same changes at the same time without Investors. Among smaller companies, the differences were particularly marked: 97 per cent of recognized companies with 10 to 50 employees measured the effectiveness of training, compared to only 49 per cent of those not involved. In terms of overall business performance, 87 per cent of recognized firms thought that Investors had made a direct or indirect contribution to improved performance.

These quantified results supported a wide range of anecdotal experience. Investors was seen to be particularly effective in increasing staff involvement, morale and commitment. In schools and universities, it provided training for non-academic staff who had often not been included in training programmes. Among retailers, it had significantly increased the involve-ment of part-time staff. In many cases, the experience of hearing back from staff their understanding of organizational purpose had led to more open and consultative forms of decision-making.

Attempts have been made to contrast Investors and non-Investors firms in terms of profitability. A study in 1995 compared 2,300 recognized firms with others in their sectors, on a range of financial measures. It concluded that the performance of recognized firms 'represents an observed performance 61 per cent better than would be expected if there was no difference between IIP recognized companies and their non-recognized competitors'. Causality is, of course, always difficult to prove. It does at least suggest a high correlation between Investors and superior performance.

Negative experiences

Negative experiences of Investors are fewer, and are mostly anecdotal. The evidence suggests that such experiences often arise from a cynical or inappropriate application of the Standard, or from a misunderstanding of what the Standard can and cannot achieve. The IES survey quoted the managing director of one company that had ceased to be involved:

> We paid lip service to the process and paid an agency to produce an action plan and had initial meetings with staff. However, when I took over the company I stopped it. I thought that for the benefits of the company I'd rather invest in capital equipment, the realities of the business.

Staff in that firm could reasonably have become cynical through their experience. The story also reveals a curiously old-fashioned approach to management: most managers today believe that staff are very much 'the realities of the business'. Managers who do not believe this remain a major problem in Britain's workplaces.

Investors can seem different depending on your position in an organization and the extent to which the Standard is associated with often necessary organizational change. A churchgoer in the Diocese of Ripon, who had applied Investors in his firm, commented: 'Now I know why my staff felt nervous.' As a manager, he was using Investors to achieve change. As a parishioner, he saw change in a different light. Managing change is a challenge that every organization faces, and it is almost impossible without dissent. A fair comparison here is not between change and stability, but between different approaches to change. The evidence that Investors increases morale suggests that it can be a good way of managing change, but very much as a framework. Poorly applied Investors projects can be experienced as coercive, the more so because of the claims implicit in the title.

Another criticism is that Investors makes no real difference. Part of the work of the Task Group was to ask members of General Synod for their experiences and opinions of Investors. One respondent, who had experienced the Standard as Chair of Governors at a school, commented:

> It did not get to the root of things, either personally or institutionally. In the end the process was pretty banal and just said nice things about the school – not all appropriate. We passed – but can one fail?

In fact, though no-one does fail, 20 per cent of organizations that apply for recognition are deferred for further work. There are cases where assessment has undoubtedly been experienced as banal.

Questions of paperwork also loom large, and reveal the balance that must be struck between exhaustive (and potentially onerous) assessment and user-friendly (and potentially inadequate) assessment. One respondent wrote:

> Consensus of opinion is that the idea sounds good on its own, but when set against the educational scene in general it appears as more bureaucracy at a time when those involved are already stressed by information overload.

This is a real experience, but must be set against the benefits claimed for staying the course.

Some people have experienced the distressing situation in which, shortly after gaining Investors, their firm was obliged to make staff redundant. 'So much for investing in people' is the easy response. But the fair question to ask is how the situation would have differed had Investors not been attempted. It is unrealistic to expect a standard largely concerned with training and development to resolve major changes in an organization's markets.

Listening to these experiences is important, not least because they do not appear at all in material published by IIPUK. To omit them is to sell Investors short. No technique applied in 30,000 organizations could possibly succeed in every one of them. A technique that allows for substantial variation in local application is particularly likely to reveal positive and negative experiences. Positive experiences outnumbered negative ones in the Task Group's survey of General Synod, and this is borne out by statistical evidence. The balance is perhaps struck by two further comments from Synod members. One puts the negative first, and the other the positive:

> IIP does not work in an organization that is unsure of itself and its direction. It is all too easy to go through the motions, get the award, but change little. If you cannot reach hearts and minds and change them, the exercise appears a waste of effort.

> Given the correct structure and support/resources, I believe this has the potential to be useful and positive for all concerned. Unfortunately, we seem to have fallen into all the potholes.

It is fair to conclude that applying Investors in a superficial way is worse than not applying it. The overwhelming proportion of negative experiences arise from that avoidable situation, or from circumstances which Investors was not designed to deal with. They do not outweigh the preponderantly positive picture.

Developments in the Standard

Interpreting experience of the Standard is complicated by the fact that it has undergone some changes since its introduction in 1991. The most concrete, but least significant, change was a clarification of its wording in 1995. More significant has been the developing debate over the unity of the Standard and the diversity of its application. The principles involved will be immediately understandable to Anglicans!

In the first phase of Investors' application, TECs took very different approaches to its promotion, to the training and selection of advisers, and to the interpretation of the Standard. IIPUK was not formed as a national guarantor of the Standard until 1993, when it began issuing guidance notes in areas of the Standard in which interpretation had varied. Assessors had always been trained to a national syllabus, but adviser training varied significantly, as did the standard of advisers. In 1997, IIPUK set about a process of training advisers to a single national syllabus. In most areas, advisers are now registered on a regional rather than local basis.

These measures improved consistency, but increased bureaucracy, complexity and cost. For example, seven criteria were developed to guide assessors over whether subsidiary parts of organizations possessed the necessary 'authority and autonomy' to commit to the Standard. In due course, the trend towards consistency reached its natural limit, and in 1998 new guidelines moved the Standard towards more flexible, locally determined interpretation. The criteria for authority and autonomy, for example, were abandoned, and the decision about the level at which a subsidiary could commit to the Standard was left to the organization concerned, provided there was some overall framework.

A number of elements enabled this relaxation. The training of advisers and assessors was complete, providing a natural ground for consistency. A network of 'internal verifiers' had been created to moderate their work. Guidance had been produced in a number of different sectors, of which this 'church sector' book is an example. IIPUK was also obliged to accede to requests that assessment be more focused on continuous improvement, and less on formal evaluation. For example, rolling annual re-assessment reports now tend to be delivered immediately and verbally, and followed up in writing.

Changes have also occurred in the role of 'recognition panels'. These are bodies composed of senior employers appointed by the local TEC. Until 1998, their job was to decide on the award of Investors to each and every organization. The process was objective, but somewhat costly and complex. Decisions on recognition will now rest with assessors, and recognition panels will moderate their decisions.

Investors has evolved, and will evolve. Some concerns about it undoubtedly refer to an earlier phase, and have already been resolved. To engage with Investors is not to adopt a fixed structure. Rather, it is to engage with an evolving process by which organizations of every kind work out how to improve their planning, training and evaluation. Participants in Investors both gain from and contribute to the process. The extent of the Standard's adoption by UK organizations suggests that people see it as a concrete way by which they can engage with the human possibilities of organizations in the modern world.

Other standards

Investors is not the only standard that organizations can seek. Another major standard, dealing with quality systems, is ISO9001 (formerly BS5750). The Quality in Ministry group, based in Nottingham, has been active in identifying means by which 'documented quality systems' can be applied to ministry.

ISO9001 and Investors are consistent, the one (in shorthand) dealing with systems, the other with the people who operate them. ISO9001 has found its greatest application in engineering and manufacturing companies, while Investors has proved most useful in organizations that are dependent on people. Many modern manufacturers have, for that reason, achieved both standards, while 'people-based' organizations have not always found a value in ISO9001.

Building on both Investors and ISO9001 is the Business Excellence Model. This is a complex model embracing leadership, people management, policy, processes, customer satisfaction, impact on society and business results. It is very much the 'gold card' among standards – though, strictly speaking, it is not a 'standard' but, rather, a self-assessment process allied to competitive awards for excellence. A group in the voluntary sector has recommended Quality Standards in the Voluntary Sector based on this model. In practice, this is a stage in organizational improvement beyond Investors. Organizations which have not achieved Investors are unlikely to score well with it, and are likely to find its multiple demands daunting.

Inevitably, other standards will be promoted, and Investors is unlikely to last for ever. However, the evidence is that it is growing to maturity rather than old age. The Standard will be nine years old in 2000. ISO9001 will be 25 years old. The support given to Investors by the present Government suggests that it has many years to run. Even then, the principles will outlast it. The Investors plaque and logo may one day become obsolete, but not the cycle of improvement based on planning, training and evaluation.

Cost or investment?

The costs of undertaking Investors vary hugely. The major cost in most organizations is the staff time devoted to it. But this can be interpreted in different ways. Is the time devoted to preparing an induction programme a 'cost', or an investment in something that every organization should do, and which saves time and money in the long run? Those who have adopted Investors prefer to use the language of 'investment' rather than 'cost'. It is not possible to generalize about the amount of staff time needed to put in place the procedures and systems to meet the Investors Standard. In voluntary organizations, including churches, most of the work can be undertaken by volunteers, so no actual expenditure arises.

There are two types of external cost. The first, of consultants and advisers, can be avoided or minimized by taking advantage of free or low-cost seminars offered by TECs, and by running the process internally. Some TECs offer advisers without charge, or offer grants for employing advisers.

Second, there is the cost of assessment. This is only incurred if an organization chooses to go for recognition. Then the cost of the assessor must be met. The maximum permissible rate for an assessor is, in late 1998, £550 per day. The number of days required for a first assessment varies from three, for organizations of up to 50 staff, to ten or more for large organizations. Some TECs offer free or subsidized assessment to voluntary organizations, and others allow reductions for small organizations.

The cost of assessment has been a major concern of the Task Group. There is clear evidence that external assessment is of great value to churches. The problem is the cost. Our proposed solution is described in Chapter 6.

2

Experience of Investors in the Church

Investors began to be used in a number of parts of the Church in 1994, less than three years after the launch of the Standard. The initiatives were entirely separate, and it was not until the creation of our Task Group in 1997 that experiences were pooled. Collectively, the Church has nearly five years' experience of working with Investors in a variety of different settings. This chapter summarizes what that experience has been in a single parish, among staff of a diocesan office, in a cathedral and in a whole diocese. The four stories cover every level and almost every type of structure in the Church. They represent a considerable geographical and demographic spread, from Somerset to Leeds, and from cathedral close to urban estate. Those who began working with Investors in 1994 were pioneers, and in all cases did things that they would have done differently in retrospect. Their work has been invaluable to our Task Group, and provides a solid basis on which the wider Church can assess the contribution that Investors can make to its life and work.

St Barnabas, Lenton Abbey

The parish of St Barnabas, Lenton Abbey, is a few miles from the centre of Nottingham, on the edge of the city and its commuter suburbs. It has a population of 3,600, living mostly in a 1930s council estate or in a few streets of semi-detached private houses. For many years, St Barnabas was joined to the nearby parish of St Mary's. Its vicarage was boarded up and, by the early 1990s, its congregation had dwindled to 25.

In 1994, the Diocese of Southwell made a commitment to rebuild the parish. A graft of members from a city-centre church was anticipated, but did not materialize. The task of the new vicar, Phil Williams, was not made easier when an arsonist burned down the parish hall and a quinquennial inspection revealed the need for a complete rewiring of the church.

Investors appeared on the scene as an initiative with fifteen local churches, supported by Greater Nottingham TEC. Phil Williams comments:

Investors dropped into our laps just as we were beginning to carve out our vision. There was an expectancy of change in the church. The key people were committed to creating a local church, and there was a willingness to have a go.

The reaction from the PCC was lukewarm. One PCC member recalls voting against the initiative, based on his experience of Investors at work: 'We'd been told to do it by head office. We just seemed to get the paperwork, and they got the training.' Another remembers: 'I thought, what on earth are we doing this for? It's a thing you associate with business.' But most people were prepared to put their misgivings aside: 'I was cynical about it, because of the paperchase there'd been at work. But Phil wanted to do it, so we gave it a go.'

During 1995 the church firmed up its aim 'to be the church in Lenton Abbey', and identified ten objectives in its mission statement. It grouped these into three:

GOALS FOR 1996
- restore the parish centre;
- make worship more accessible;
- increase the sense of belonging.

The plan looks very different from a traditional business plan. It is written on a sheet of A3 paper, in a series of boxes linked to the aim of the church. Goals lead on to targets, and those in turn to the people who would be responsible and the training they would need to do the job. Investors requires 'a written but flexible plan' that 'sets out the organization's goals and targets' (Indicator 2.1). A handwritten A3 sheet pinned up at the back of church can meet that requirement as well as a 50-page bound document. It also provides an accessible way for people to see how their work fits into the overall plan.

A major element in Investors is training. The parish reader commented:

> I used to go on courses and go to conferences. Someone might have known I'd gone, but there was no chance to talk about it. I wanted it to be for the whole church. Now I'm always asked how it has gone, and what I learned, and I'm encouraged to share.

An early task was to renew the rota of sidespeople, and this was accompanied by a list of things to do and a briefing session. 'It didn't seem as formal as training, but you know what you've got to do', a member of the rota remarked.

Elaine Hinchliffe took on the job of Training and Development Co-ordinator. She found it hard-going at first: 'It was difficult to get hold of because of the jargon and because I wasn't used to the management side of things. It took six months for the penny to drop.' Her report for 1996–7 identifies eighteen separate pieces of training, involving more than 50 people, and ranging from first aid to Celtic spirituality, and from mini-bus driving to Bible study. The total cost was £227.

The question of what it meant 'to be the church in Lenton Abbey' was explored in parallel to this work. A sermon series in January–February 1996 was devoted to Ephesians. Phil Williams recalls: 'An exploration of what it meant to be the Body of Christ was an important part of our whole theological reflection.' This focused on the whole range of developments in the parish, and not specifically on Investors. St Barnabas understood itself to be 'using' rather than 'doing' Investors.

By the end of 1996, two years after starting, Investors was well entrenched. But it was not always known as 'Investors'. Phil Williams comments: 'The action plans were for the church, and were not always flagged up as Investors.' The most visible developments were in the activity of the parish and its fabric. By 1997, about 40 people had taken one of three Alpha courses, the parish hall had been rebuilt, the rewiring was complete, and the congregation had more than doubled to 55. Parish share increased from £3,000 in 1994, which St Barnabas struggled to meet, to £12,000 in 1998, which it met in full. In October 1996, St Barnabas became the first part of any Christian church to be recognized as an Investor in People.

What lay behind this? Phil Williams is very clear where the credit must go: 'It was God and the people who did it. Investors was a channel; it was not the substance.' Looking at it from a different perspective, the Investors assessor also placed primary emphasis on people and their motivation:

> St Barnabas Church has worked very hard over the last two years to set in place a series of organizational changes to secure the operation and success for the future. Investors in People has been part of the framework employed to enhance this and this work has not only contributed towards the achievement of the National Standard but has given enthusiasm and hope to everyone concerned. Everyone interviewed, without exception, felt that the future could now

be approached with enthusiasm and that the processes in place could only support any changes or events to come.

Feelings in the parish had certainly changed. The PCC member who had voted against Investors commented:

> It's a godsend. It stops the woolly thinking that it'll be all right on the night. We don't get lost as we used to do. It helps us look at what we really need to do, frees time up. It's our fault if we don't use it well.

Whether this could have happened without Investors is impossible to tell. The IES survey quoted in Chapter 1 found that 85 per cent of Investors companies felt that the changes they had achieved would not have happened at the same time without Investors. This seems to be the picture at St Barnabas. One PCC member comments: 'Investors gave us the impetus to get started. We'd probably have found some other method if it wasn't there, but it was.' Another says: 'I don't know if we'd have done it without Investors.'

Acquiring the Investors plaque was celebrated, but in a low-key way. The plaque did not appear on the wall for another year, because the faculty to install it was bundled with a number of other matters for the Diocesan Advisory Committee. The Investors logo has never appeared on the St Barnabas letterhead. So was it worthwhile going for assessment? Phil Williams is convinced it was. He argues: 'Assessment stops you fooling yourself. It provides an objective measure, and it keeps you going when you might give up.'

St Barnabas is due for re-assessment in October 1999. The real test then will be how Investors thinking has entered the life of the church. 'It's like wine fermenting, or like an unwieldy snowball that perhaps Investors can guide,' says Phil Williams. 'Increasingly, I see Investors as identifying what people need, to enable them to do what God is calling them to do. With new people coming into the church and circumstances changing, it's a never-ending task.'

The diocesan staff, Bath and Wells

The Diocese of Bath and Wells covers Somerset and some surrounding areas. It has 500 parishes, 250 clergy and an electoral roll of 30,000. Investors has not so far been approached at a parish level. Rather, it has focused on the diocesan staff – the diocesan office, the bishop and his suffragan, the two archdeacons and their support staff, and some resource ministers who are also parish clergy. Together, these can be called 'the diocesan staff', and amount to some 50 people. They are, in the words of Nick Denison, the Diocesan Secretary, 'the people whose principal function is to serve the parishes'.

Senior members of the diocesan office began to look at Investors in 1994. The initiative came from the education department, a substantial operation with a turnover of £400,000, a £2m capital budget and eleven full-time equivalent staff. The then director recalls: 'There was no system of people or resource management. People just did their own thing.' Nick Denison remembers that his first reaction to Investors was that: 'It seems a lot of hard work.' A colleague had experienced it in her previous work, and had mixed views about it. On closer enquiry, Nick Denison felt Investors would 'help do things I'd wanted to do for a long time, mainly practical things like recruitment policy, job descriptions and using the computer networks, but also to do with culture, helping us to find a way of seeing ourselves as part of a corporate structure'.

The initiative dovetailed with an exploration of diocesan aims instituted by Jim Thompson, who became bishop in 1991. The diocesan mission, to 'go for God', and the ten aims drawn from it were widely distributed in the diocese. It was increasingly clear that, if the aims were to be carried through, there needed to be more cohesive management of diocesan resources, a clearer sense of purpose, and better training and evaluation. 'We believe this is crucial to our future success in promoting the mission of the church,' the Chairman of the Diocesan Board of Finance told the local paper when the diocese committed to achieve the Investors Standard in January 1995.

The diagnosis of the diocesan office, based at the Old Deanery, showed just how much work there was to do. The initial responses of one senior manager to statements based on the Investors indicators are typical:

> 'Our most senior staff are committed to developing people.'
> – Enthusiasm shown in many quarters, but no policy or structure in place to fulfil promises.

> 'The Diocese has defined its broad aims or vision.' – The ten aims are in existence but there's no evidence of a detailed business plan amplifying the aims into a more functional document.

> 'Our training and development plans are effectively implemented.' – There are no training and development plans as far as I am aware.

'We evaluate how our investment in people is contributing to our goals and targets.' – Not demonstrated at the Old Deanery as no mechanism available – no appraisal process in place.

Just under three years later, Jan Hill, the Somerset TEC adviser assigned to the diocese, conducted an interim review. She found that: 'There was universal agreement, supported by the staff survey, that communications had been improved.' She found in relation to diocesan purpose that: 'Staff understand the purpose of the Diocese as defined within the Ten Aims. Most of those interviewed were aware of what they were expected to contribute to the success of the Diocese.'

Concrete steps had been taken in a number of areas. An appraisal system had been introduced in 1995 and, following experience, revised in 1998. A Development Plan had been written in January 1997, identifying more than a hundred 'key actions' under the headings of the ten aims, the great majority of those actions for completion in 1997. Job descriptions had been introduced for all staff. In the education department, a structured performance-based evaluation system had been introduced. Communication within the diocesan office had been improved with a monthly staff newsletter and regular staff meetings. An induction programme had been introduced in 1995 and a staff handbook written. Staff training and development activities were being recorded, and all department heads had a budget with an allocation for training.

The bishop commented: 'Investors has made me deal with the realities of my staff's lives, and it's been a revelation to me.' He cited improvements in setting goals, evaluating performance, and communications as major benefits. But two major problems remained. The first goes to the heart of the operation of a diocese, and the second relates to the treatment of theological questions.

In her review, Jan Hill pointed out: 'There's a lack of a central linchpin with the time or skill to plan and evaluate and to integrate it operationally.' This comment pinpoints the reasons Nick Denison had for embarking on the process in the first place: the need 'to find a way of seeing ourselves as part of a corporate structure'. The problem is not readily resolvable. The 1997 Development Plan mentioned above, led by Richard Lewis, now Bishop of St Edmundsbury and Ipswich, was difficult to assemble, and even more difficult to implement. The lack of an overarching plan does not preclude progress, but it makes it more difficult. Jan Hill argues: 'You can get to recognition even without a strategic and operational linchpin. It's possible to do it with a patchwork of practices which only later make sense.'

In an interview about Investors with the local paper in 1995, Bishop Jim said: 'I am quite sure that if Jesus Christ had been around today he would have signed up to it.' Not everyone was so convinced. Significant resistance came from those who questioned the project on theological grounds. One staff member commented: 'It's relatively easy to say that Investors accords with the whole Christian ethos of the place, and Jim picked up on that immediately. But I couldn't argue it on theological grounds – I'd be lost.' Another member of staff said: 'We've never really looked at it theologically. We've been pragmatic.' The absence of theological discussion meant that the Bath and Wells project did not enjoy the support of all staff. The grounds on which, we suggest, Investors can be evaluated from a theological perspective are discussed in Chapter 3.

The diocesan staff in Bath and Wells tackled a more complex challenge than the people of St Barnabas, and it is not surprising that there is still some way to go before they meet the Standard. It is important to set this in context. One staff member commented:

> Before Nick came, the style was cold and bureaucratic, with no focus on people. Investors was really an extension of Nick's change in style, towards a concern for people and their training. But we underestimated the resource block at the beginning. Apart from the education department, we were coming from nowhere.

Lichfield Cathedral

Lichfield Cathedral is the centre of one of England's biggest dioceses, and it is also one of the country's less frequently visited cathedrals, located in a small West Midlands town just off the A38 between Derby and Birmingham. Like most cathedrals, Lichfield faces a number of challenges: the implementation of the Cathedrals Measure, the impact of health and safety and other legislation, the costs of the choir, the management of visitors, and the role of the cathedral congregation and its place in diocesan life. By any measure, cathedrals present a significant management challenge.

David Wallington was appointed as Chief Executive Officer in 1995, an enhanced job from that of the administrator who preceded him. He came from a civil service background, where he had been used to specialist support in a variety of areas. He had come across Investors peripherally, but in this new context it appeared to offer a useful tool. The issue was focused when the Head Steward raised the question of training for vergers. How, with available skills and resources, was this to be tackled? Investors, David Wallington felt, provided a structure and source of expertise that could help him make the changes necessary at the cathedral.

The chapter had prepared a document, 'Strategy 2000', but no work had been undertaken to implement it. David Wallington's early objectives were to focus the role of chapter meetings on policy and evaluation, and to create a management structure reporting to them. From there, he aimed to develop job descriptions for staff, to institute appraisals, to write a policy for volunteers and to introduce an induction programme for people new to the cathedral. He recalls:

> I could easily have put all this on the back burner and said 'This is too much trouble.' But I didn't want to leave it as I found it to my successor. Investors puts a structure in place that will survive all of us.

The application of Investors was strongly supported by the Dean, Tom Wright, who argues: 'If a theological rationale for cathedrals exists, it follows that we must make the fullest use of our gifts to carry it out.'

A diagnosis of the cathedral against the Investors indicators was completed in 1997. In spring 1998, Staffordshire TEC funded three workshops for the dean and chapter and department heads to explore the way forward. The first workshop identified roles, responsibilities and reporting structures. The second developed twelve objectives for the cathedral and elaborated a model for a 'business plan' to put them into effect. The third brought the responsibilities and objectives together, and identified both barriers to be overcome and factors that would enable the plan to proceed.

By late 1998, progress had been made primarily with clarifying objectives and organizing the management structure. Much remained to be done, but practical changes had also followed. The managers of the bookshop and café, for example, now operated with devolved budgets and were responding with their own initiatives. David Wallington recalls that resistance was considerable at first, for example to meetings of departmental heads:

> I worked in the civil service for 25 years, and when consultants came in there, people said: 'We're different.' When I came here they said the same, and I said: 'Oh really?' Now we're seeing change, and it's accepted.

The Diocese of Ripon

The Diocese of Ripon covers Leeds and the central part of North Yorkshire, stretching north to the borders of Durham. Demographically, it is a microcosm of the UK population, with its combination of financial services and urban poverty, comfortable villages and rural uplands. It has a population of 730,000, and 268 churches gathered in 158 parishes. There are 26,000 people on its electoral registers.

The impetus for Investors arose from questions posed by deanery synods about the cost and structure of the diocese. These in turn raised other questions. What direction should the diocese take, and what structures would it need? What work would best be done at diocesan and what at deanery level? What support did parishes need? Senior staff in the diocese were wrestling with these questions in mid-1994 when a member of the diocesan office attended an Investors seminar. Investors appeared to offer a way to approach the questions.

In particular, Investors moved the focus away from structures and towards determining the aims of the diocese and developing plans and skills so that people could share in trying to achieve those aims. Senior clergy spoke of diocesan policy-making as 'a reactive process that responds to perceived pastoral need', of the diocese 'not working well', and of senior staff as 'not a team, but a group of individuals with specialist roles and agendas and personalities that occasionally clash'. It was recognized that structures alone were not at the root of the problem. Rather, it was the lack of shared purpose, and the lack of an integrated plan to give coherence to the multi-faceted work of the diocese. Something more substantial than a reform of boards was needed, and Investors appeared to offer that.

Peter Marshall, then Director of Training in Ripon and now Dean of Worcester, described Investors as 'a good, basic educational model, an action learning approach'. John Holmes, Diocesan Missioner in Ripon and now Wakefield, saw Investors as the means by which best mission practice could be spread, and the diocese as a whole could move 'from maintenance to mission'. The challenge, however, was that no-one had any experience of using Investors in the Church, least of all on the scale of a complete diocese.

The approach adopted was to start with a single deanery, and with a workbook on parish audit and planning. This closely resembled parish audit and planning initiatives described by John Finney and others (1991). The difference was that it was conducted simultaneously for a whole deanery, and with specific reference to the inter-relations between parish, deanery and diocese. The diocese committed to this pilot project, funded by Leeds TEC, in October 1994.

The pilot Whitkirk deanery comprises fifteen parishes in the east of Leeds, a combination of inner-city, suburban and rural fringe. During the autumn, facilitators were trained in the use of the workbook and the basic principles of Investors. In the spring, each congregation appointed a team to undertake the workbook over four evenings. It covered the identification of strengths, weaknesses, opportunities and threats (SWOT), the preparation of a statement of mission, the selection of three objectives for the coming year and their elaboration into plans, and an evaluation of what the parish could both gain from and contribute to deanery and diocese. A congregational survey was also carried out, and census data supplied for each parish.

Later in the spring, PCCs considered the proposals of their project teams. They were then gathered together for the deanery as a whole, and a synod and then a deanery conference were devoted to hammering out a strategy for the deanery. Facilitators who had helped parish groups formed the basis of a deanery project team to take the process forward.

The process was well received. Every parish participated, and 137 people were involved in project teams. In the follow-up assessment, participants recommended by a margin of four to one that the process be applied elsewhere. The diocese agreed to this, and the process was extended to the whole diocese in autumn 1995. It was to involve over 80 facilitators, more than a thousand members of project teams, and the participation of 80 per cent of the parishes. By the summer of 1996, the diocese had summarized on database the SWOT analysis, mission statement and objectives of 190 parishes or congregations, the great majority of the total.

Rural deans met in May 1996 to consider the results, and the mood was upbeat. 'What we're looking at is a totally new culture in how the church goes about its business,' commented one. Another said: 'We're moving into Trinitarian thinking, understanding our inter-dependence.' A third said: 'I'm delighted to be surprised. I thought it was a complete non-starter in my deanery.' Actions reported included a deanery conference in Ripon, a deanery newsletter in Wensley, the use of synod in Allerton as a 'marketplace' for parish ideas and solutions, and reports by facilitators on parish responses at other deanery synods. Analysis by resource ministers identified specific needs in mission support, liturgy, youth work and other areas that were followed up with the parishes concerned.

This was a large-scale project, but it was far from unique. It has similarities with, for example, the 'Agenda for Action' launched by David Hope in

London in 1992 and 'The Way Forward' launched in Manchester by Christopher Mayfield in 1994. Both these engaged parishes in mission planning on a consistent basis. Neither was known to those planning the Ripon project in 1994–5, a characteristic of church initiatives that will be explored in Chapter 4. The difference with the Ripon project was that parish planning there was only the first phase of a cyclical process built on the Investors model.

The aims were for planning and evaluation at diocesan, deanery and parish level to become parts of a single, inter-related cycle, and for the development of people to be at the heart of that cycle. To that end, the diocese adopted a series of measures during 1995–6. It issued a mission statement, created a Policy Co-ordination Group to bring together finance and policy in Bishop's Council, developed an appraisal system for lay staff, reviewed the operation of episcopal visits, and began to look at the resourcing of and delegation of authority to deaneries. It also began to look at drawing up its budgets on the basis of plans, rather than by carrying forward expenditure from the previous year.

In spring 1997, the diocese held a conference for more than 500 clergy and laity from the great majority of parishes. This sought to bring together the plans that parishes had set out and the steps the diocese had taken to meet the needs expressed by them. It launched a process for parishes to review the progress they had made with their plans, and to specify new targets for the following year. It also moved the focus towards the identification of training needs and the development of training policies. Now that plans had been set out, it was possible to look more closely at the training needed to put them into effect.

The conference revealed that the challenge facing the diocese was deeper than had been anticipated. Distrust of the intentions of the diocese ran deep. Descriptions of changes that had taken place (such as the creation of the Policy Co-ordination Group) cut little ice. Many parishes were resistant to the idea that they needed training in evaluation and then later did not understand how to undertake evaluation. The conference demonstrated that challenges as identified in 1994 could not be resolved by a single cycle of planning and evaluation. Shifting to a genuinely shared vision for the diocese, and an integrated effort to put it into effect, would be a long haul.

Nevertheless, half the parishes in the diocese completed their evaluation forms, and their responses were again put on a database and shared with deaneries and resource ministers. Major initiatives, such as deanery resourcing and lay appraisal, continued. In many parishes, Investors took root, and became part of the fabric of their life. At diocesan level, Investors principles began to be reflected in the emphasis given to training as a component of diocesan life. In April 1997, a Commission on the future leadership of the diocese commented:

> The 'Investors in People' initiative has been widely valued at all levels of diocesan life. It is important that the fruits of the exercise should not be lost. It is particularly important that there should be a vital and active link between the vision of the diocese and that of each local Christian community. We recommend that the 'Investors in People' initiative be continued and encouraged in every aspect of parish, deanery and diocesan life.

The Investors project in Ripon had been jointly funded by Leeds TEC and Leeds Church Institute. This funding, which paid for a consultant to work with the diocesan Project Team in its first three years, came to an end in summer 1997. A new Director of Training was appointed, who was unwilling to take on his predecessor's role as Internal Project Manager. The diocese then disbanded the Project Team so that Investors could be carried forward by existing structures, headed by Bishop's Council. It sought to integrate Investors with its ongoing work. This proved more difficult than had been envisaged.

A follow-up seminar on Investors in spring 1998 re-established enthusiasm for the process. A Task Force chaired by the Archdeacon of Leeds was formed to identify the next steps. It proposed that 'the Investors process should cease to be treated as an initiative in its own right, but rather as a tool to assist the diocese'. It could, for example, help determine the role of area deans and assist a new project entitled 'Deanery Resources for Mission', which required deaneries to identify mission opportunities and the resources to meet them. At a local level parishes and deaneries continue in their own particular work towards the Standard.

Other Anglican Investors projects

Organizations become involved with Investors at a local level, and do not appear on a national list until they have been recognized. The statistics unit of Investors in People UK uses the Standard Industrial Classification for sector groups and does not currently have specific coding for voluntary, charity and religious organizations. Any list of church Investors projects is therefore likely to be incomplete. Within the Anglican Communion, other dioceses which have indicated that they are using or planning to use

Investors are the Diocese of Bangor in the Church in Wales and the diocesan offices in the Dioceses of Blackburn, Sheffield and Lichfield. The United Society for the Propagation of the Gospel decided in 1995 not to make use of Investors, but may re-visit it in the future. The Upside Down Trust (formerly Scripture Union Training and Development Unit) was uncertain about Investors' potential for a broad-based organization. The Board of Education and the National Society are aware of a number of church schools that have been recognized or are making use of Investors.

Investors in other churches and denominations

Responses to our enquiries were received from:

- the United Reformed Church national office – not aware of any developments;

- the Methodist Church Open Learning Centre – has looked into Investors in a number of quarters but so far no commitment has been made;

- the Religious Society of Friends in Britain – does not feel it is appropriate;

- the Salvation Army, Brighowgate House, Grimsby – see below.

In October 1994 the Salvation Army made an Investors commitment to the Humberside TEC. This would focus on the training and development of all employees and on achieving the business goals and targets of Brighowgate House, a social service centre for men and women, accommodating 60 people. The Management Team communicated to all employees its vision for the centre and of the contribution each person could make. This led to a more precise definition of job roles, and highlighted the importance of good induction, staff appraisals, ongoing review of progress, and evaluation of all training and development activities against the centre's goals and targets. A very important part of the work done was the formation of a Steering Committee, with representation from each work team – management, catering, cleaning and administration.

The Officer-in-Charge, Michael Matson, feels that the improved teamworking has enhanced the service offered to the residents of the centre. Staff members are much more aware of how their particular contribution affects the work of colleagues and thus the running of the centre. It is rare for anyone now to say 'That is not my job.' Humberside TEC recognized the Salvation Army, Brighowgate House, as an Investor in People in September 1996.

YMCA Training (part of the National Council of YMCAs) achieved the Investors Standard in 1995 and a number of associations are working towards it. They feel that it has sharpened up their planning and evaluation processes and that, in a local setting, it is a good tool to encourage lifelong learning.

Some conclusions

The above experiences of Investors in the Church are important evidence for the recommendations the Task Group has been asked to make. A full assessment requires theological evaluation, which is the subject of the next chapter. Meanwhile a number of conclusions can be drawn:

● In every case, Investors was experienced as providing positive benefits, particularly where it was pursued consistently.

● It is easier to achieve the Standard in a short time period in a single parish than among diocesan staff, let alone in a complete diocese. Yet, for Anglicans, the single parish is not the limit of the Church.

● The challenge of relating together within a diocese has nowhere proved amenable to simple solutions.

● In all cases, Investors was introduced in response to real and often complex challenges. In no case did it offer an off-the-shelf solution. Rather, it drew out the true nature of the challenges and caused them to be faced.

● Investors obliged those involved to address fundamental questions of purpose, and had the effect of drawing them to closer reflection on what God is calling the Church to be.

● Participation in Investors has invariably been resisted by some, if not the majority, of those asked to engage with it. Yet those who have persisted with it cite benefits which entirely accord with those claimed by other organizations.

● The management of change is a challenge for all organizations. As a means of carrying out change, Investors has proved to have significant benefits in the Church as in other organizations.

3

Theological Evaluation

It is part of Christian believing to ask of any proposed measure whether the church with theological integrity can adopt it. Theological evaluation is thus not just an option in an assessment of Investors, but central to the Christian approach to it. That evaluation must be based on a balanced reading of the text of the Standard, on an understanding of the principles behind it and on experience of its application, just as it must be based on a balanced reading of Scripture and knowledge of Christian tradition.

Theological evaluation also enables a proposal to be intelligently owned by a whole church. It is made necessary by the nature of church as the community of faith. In St Barnabas, the process of evaluating Investors was aided by being placed within an examination of what it means to be the Body of Christ. In Bath and Wells, the lack of theological discussion meant that legitimate questions about the appropriateness of the Standard were associated with resistance. To discuss Investors theologically does not mean that acceptance will automatically follow. It does mean that the grounds for rejection or acceptance can be heard and respected, if not shared. This evaluation will begin with the case for Investors, before going on to consider theological objections to it.

The theological case for Investors

Any proposal for the ordering of the Church's life, of which Investors is one, must be grounded in the nature of the community called into being by the saving action of God in Christ. That in turn must be grounded in the belief that Scripture holds all things necessary for salvation. As Colin Buchanan observes:

> If this principle is taken seriously, then Anglicans need to root their doctrine of the Church in Scripture and to be ready to adjust their self-understanding, their universal ecclesiology, and their way of life and practice in accordance with Scripture. (Buchanan, 1998)

However, that is easier said than done. Buchanan notes a number of difficulties. Interpreting the few direct scriptural references to the Church is not easy. It is not clear that biblical writers were addressing the questions of church order that we try to ask, or that texts can bear the weight we put on them. There is extensive dispute about what biblical material is relevant, and an enormous capacity to draw conflicting conclusions from the same texts. History has given us a large number of denominations, whose self-understanding has become inseparable from particular readings of the biblical evidence. And whereas in central areas of faith the early Church reached solid conclusions that have formed the basis of Christian orthodoxy, in ecclesiology the practice was divergent and theology followed that divergence.

All ecclesiology is thus to some extent 'derived', the adjective Buchanan uses to talk about the New Testament evidence. It would be a poor ecclesiology that did not take account of central Christian doctrines of incarnation, atonement and Trinity. It would be inadequate if it did not deal both with the images of Church in the New Testament and with the history of the early Church, which often bear little relationship to each other. And it would fail if, in pursuing specifically ecclesiological questions, it did not constantly refer beyond them to God's mission expressed in the whole of creation and in all human history. Ecclesiology is not open to a simple, linear argument from text or doctrine. It must be derived from a balanced reading of all these factors.

For this reason, the Task Group has avoided simple, but ultimately misleading, justifications for the application of Investors. A central concern of Investors is planning. Does this have a scriptural basis? It could be argued that Jesus uses the analogy of planning for war or for building a tower as an analogy for the Christian life (Luke 14.28-32). It could be said that the sending out of the disciples represents a prototype mission plan (Matthew 10.5-15), and that Paul's journeys were masterpieces of organization. Such an approach is opportunist. It trivializes Scripture and makes use of highly selective reading of texts, such as the 'Petrine' text (Matthew 16.18) to justify Renaissance concepts of papacy. Ecumenical progress in this century has depended on the willingness of denominations to modify such selective readings. It would be wrong to reintroduce them.

The essential case for Investors, as for any other proposal, is that, *at this particular point in history, and in the light of the particular situation of the Church of England, it offers possibilities for the Church to be closer to what God calls it to be.* In the absence of simple, linear arguments we believe that this case is best made by approaching the subject from a number of different and complementary perspectives. We offer three perspectives. The first asks whether Investors gives concrete form to the Trinitarian ground of the Church. The second explores Investors in the light of the Body of Christ. The third asks whether the experience of applying Investors shows evidence that the fruits of the Spirit are present.

Giving concrete form to Trinitarian ecclesiology

The theological introduction to the Turnbull Report on the central structures of the Church of England states:

> The Church is the body of those who believe in the Son, and, as his bride, is the object of the Son's own love. We live out of the resources which God in his love has promised and given, by the Holy Spirit shed abroad in the hearts of the faithful. The life of the Church, in a rich and yet mysterious way, is thus utterly Trinitarian in its ground, hope and being. (Archbishops' Commission, 1995)

Similar thinking is central to the theological statement by the House of Bishops on Eucharistic Presidency. It acknowledges that to derive an ecclesiology directly from God's Trinitarian life carries both risk and difficulty. It continues:

> Nevertheless, while recognising that it is hazardous to think of any doctrine of the Trinity providing a simple blueprint for ecclesiology, it belongs to the heart of the Christian faith that God, through self-revelation in Christ, has invited us to know him as he eternally is, as irreducibly triune. (House of Bishops, 1997)

If the life and action of the Church are grounded in the life and action of this triune God, then our ecclesiology of necessity requires some deliberate attention to Trinitarian doctrine.

Central to this is the relatedness of Christians as equals in baptism, in a dynamic community that discerns and participates in God's mission. That community is rooted in, but not exhausted by, the local worshipping congregation. It expresses God's mission in the concrete and specific, in a particular historic situation, and necessarily with human skill and judgement. And it remains for ever under the judgement of God, whose purposes can never be wholly captured by human insight. Three points follow from this.

- *First, the process of discerning God's purpose is a communal rather than an individual act.* A church which is not constantly asking what God is calling it to do is not truly open to God. Since perspectives differ, this seeking of purpose is necessarily controversial, provisional and difficult. It is tempting to leave it to church leaders, subverting the equality of all believers, or to leave it to individuals, subverting the communal nature of Christian faith. It is tempting to allow purpose to remain at a level of generality so that it has no concrete reality, or simply to evade all the difficulties by not looking for a purpose at all. For these reasons, discerning God's purpose requires some process that is collective, which does not evade difficult issues, and which is reflected in concrete action.

- *Second, the Church's participation in God's mission requires some mechanism by which the gifts of all Christians can be discerned, clarified and enabled.* Without a conscious process, qualities of community and equality are lost. It is too easy for the discernment of gifts to become an individual process. It is too easy for the less confident to be unrecognized, and for their gifts to be undeveloped. The result, familiar in all congregations, is that gifts given by God remain undiscovered. For this to happen is not simply a loss of resource to the Church, important though that is. It is a failure in stewardship, a neglect of God's gracious gift.

- *Third, the results of actions taken by the Church need to be constantly referred back to God's mission.* They have no value outside that mission. Yet, in practice, church activities can take on a life of their own, undertaken because they have always been undertaken, or justified by secular need. To ask of any action whether it accords with God's purpose is not easy, particularly in a communal context where individuals may have strong personal investment in particular practices. A conscious process is required if actions are to be reflected upon in the light of God's purpose.

To make actual a Trinitarian ecclesiology, the Church needs a process which enables it to discern God's purpose, give concrete expression to it, discern and enable the gifts of all believers, and subject its practices to regular interrogation in the light of God's purpose. The process must be continuous, because the Holy Spirit is dynamic and always moving forward to the consummation of God's purpose. The process must also consciously engage the Church at local and wider level, since relatedness knows no boundaries. This suggests the need for a process that is open, transparent and shared between churches.

Realizing a Trinitarian ecclesiology does not necessarily lead to Investors, any more than it necessarily leads to synodical forms of government. There may well be better mechanisms, now or in the future. It does place an obligation on the Church to search for the mechanisms given by human reason and contemporary society which most accord with the theological imperative. This has been the process by which synodical government has evolved in the last 150 years. It expresses important theological perspectives. It also reflects secular understanding of the strengths and limitations of democratic processes in other areas of human life.

This final step in the argument requires the use of human reason. Christians have always understood that God can be seen in the secular, even when he is not acknowledged. The Church, and Israel before it, has always turned to the secular for skills and insights that faith itself, or the faith community, does not supply (see, for example, 2 Chronicles 2.7). The evidence that Investors is found to be of value in all kinds of organizations is thus of theological weight. It is this that allows one to argue that, in the present circumstances of the Church of England, Investors delivers major components of a Trinitarian ecclesiology, and is a practice that the Church can embrace.

Building the Body

Scripture offers a range of metaphors or images of the Church, of which the Body of Christ, the People of God and the Fellowship of Faith are among the powerful. These images co-exist with accounts of the achievements and defections of the early Church, of agreement and dissension and of often decisive, pragmatic steps taken to order the Church in the light of Christ (see, for example, Galatians 2.14ff). It is not possible to draw a single, concrete pattern of Church from the New Testament, but it is possible to identify what the diversity of patterns was aimed at achieving – conformity to the life and model of Christ. As the Church has sought to understand what that means, it has returned continuously to the truths that the metaphors disclose.

Metaphors for the Church are essentially organic and this is particularly true of the images used by Jesus, notably the vine (John 15.5). There is a striking contrast between this and images such as a machine or political system used to describe other organizations. The inappropriateness of those images for the Church draws attention to the need for metaphors to be grounded in reality, to be expressive of what an organization actually is. The central metaphors of the Church have an eschatological as well as a descriptive quality. When we say 'We are the Body of Christ,' we are not

simply stating that we are organically related to one another, but expressing our faith and hope in our complete incorporation in Christ.

We are obliged by this to take seriously the extent to which we are a people,
a fellowship and a body, and to bring our corporate life more fully into
accord with the metaphors we use. It is this that gives theological under-
pinning to the notion of 'the learning Church'. Learning is neither an
individual act nor an option for Christians. Nor is it a novelty. It is no
accident that the Christian Church maintained traditions of learning after
the fall of the Roman Empire, that learning was focused on monasteries
through the Middle Ages, that an open Bible in each church was a central
demand of the Reformation, and that churches took a leading role in the
expansion of education in the nineteenth century. To learn, and to do so
corporately, has always been central to the Church's self-understanding.
Professor David Ford has drawn attention to the particular need today:

> In a society that is increasingly saturated by information and
> in which lifelong learning is becoming the norm, people are
> constantly inundated by worldviews, values, beliefs,
> opinions, images and lifestyles which challenge their own. If
> we are a Church committed to being part of the drawing
> together of all things and consequently maintaining complex
> boundaries and a relatively open identity, then either,
> because of our relative openness, we are swamped and our
> people are confused or overwhelmed by very powerful and
> well-resourced forces in our culture, or we learn our faith, our
> worship, our ethics, more intelligently, more thoughtfully,
> more imaginatively and more practically: in a word, more
> wisely. And if we make it a top priority to be that sort of com-
> munity of learners, of disciples, then we will be able to offer
> a more fully habitable ecology of truth, beauty and wisdom
> to a culture that is in deep need of it. (Ford, 1998)

To 'learn our faith', as Professor Ford describes, needs some conscious
process, already evident in the substantial take-up of diocesan foundation
and bishops' certificate courses, Alpha and Emmaus courses, the growth
of lay leadership training, and the impetus to nurture given by the On The
Way report on Christian initiation. But substantial gaps remain in the level
and comprehensiveness of development, nurture and training in the
Church. Learning needs a further level of integration into our corporate life
if it is to be fully expressive of our corporate existence in Christ. Investors
offers a means of achieving this in three main ways:

- First, it asserts that training and development are for everyone in the organization, not just for leaders. This may act as some corrective to the overwhelming bias of Church training expenditure towards clergy.

- Second, it requires that training and development are evaluated at individual, team and organizational levels. This emphasizes that our learning has both an individual and a collective dimension, and that the collective exists at several levels.

- Third, it makes competence in training and development a key attribute of 'managers'. This helps give concrete form to the role of clergy and other leaders in enabling and focusing the ministry of all the baptized. This detail is expressive of the central thrust of Investors, that the development of people is at the heart of organizational success. To be more fully the Body of Christ is the 'success' that we seek, much as we regard its completion as an eschatological category. Theological reflection on the meaning of core metaphors for the Church thus leads, if not directly to Investors, at least to something very like it.

Showing the fruits of the Spirit

To argue for Investors on grounds of a Trinitarian ecclesiology is to argue from the compatibility of the inner logic, or ratio, of both Investors and Trinity. To argue for it from the nature of the Body of Christ is also to begin with concept and theory, though of a different nature. There is a third and complementary approach. That is to look at the results of Investors in the concrete situations in which it has been applied, and to ask whether it 'bears good fruit' (Matthew 7.18).

If Investors can help the Church to be more Christ-like, we should expect those parts of the Church that have used it to show the fruits of the Spirit. That, indeed, is the evidence described in Chapter 2. The story of St Barnabas is a story of a local church growing in faith and witness, of deepening nurture, and of the increasing realization of the gifts of its congregation. It is also a story of openness to its community, of service and of humility. A process that has these results can be judged to be of God.

The stories of Bath and Wells and Ripon are more complex, partly because the Investors process is far from complete, and partly because there are evident differences of opinion about the process. But it is perverse not to see the fruits of the Spirit in more than a thousand people working on parish plans across a diocese; in the perception that communications have improved in a diocesan office; and in a growing clarity on the part of individuals about how their work fits into diocesan purpose.

The notion of 'fruits' contains within it an allowance for muddle, failure and provisionality. The fruits of the Spirit – 'love, joy, peace, patience, kindness, generosity, faithfulness, gentleness, and self-control' (Galatians 5.22) – are not readily realizable. Self-control and patience remain necessary as a result, not least in Church circles. But this does not mean that the fruits of the Spirit do not form part of the promise and hope that activate our lives. The Church needs to take concrete steps to live in the promise that these fruits are part of a new humanity which is being re-made in Christ, part of his gracious gift. Anthony Thiselton has written:

> The Holy Spirit comes to be experienced in the present only as the 'first fruits' of a fuller harvest yet to come. The 'fruit' may not be fully ripe. No human person may yet be innocent of all manipulation or self-interest. Yet just as in the present the active agency of the Holy Spirit begins to reshape the self and reshape the world, so the divine Trinitarian promise of love to complete this transformation will, in turn, reshape every horizon and every interest. (Thiselton, 1995)

Living in this way requires us to look positively at the fruits we see in those parts of the Church which have used Investors. It also warns us against any superficial claim that St Barnabas, or any situation, has achieved a state of perfection that all human history warns is illusory. The claim for Investors is altogether more modest: that, in the particular circumstances of the Church of England today, it demonstrably helps God's people live and work in a way that gives some partial glimpse of his promise.

Objections to Investors

The most common ground of objection is that there is, or should be, a more spiritual way for the Church to order its life. If the Church is to be focused on God's saving action in Christ, and draw on the continual work of the Holy Spirit, it is to these resources that we should look, and not to a secular management standard. This is an overarching objection, and would put in question many practices in common use in the Church, from fire procedures to accountancy rules. Objections are put more specifically in one or more of the following four ways.

1   *Investors is part of a pattern of modern capitalism that is an affront to the gospel*

This objection looks less at the specific content of the Investors Standard than at its place within late twentieth-century capitalism. It is noted that Investors was drafted by the employers' organization, the CBI, and drew predominantly on 'best practice' within major companies. It is argued that these companies are also responsible for (or at least associated with) environmental degradation and with radical and growing disparities in wealth. Their use of 'people' language is often cynical and exploitative. To discuss Investors outside the context of the social and economic context which gave rise to it, and of which it forms a part, is to misunderstand its real nature.

The German theologian Ulrich Duchrow has argued that the global economic system represents a challenge to the fundamental nature of the gospel as strong as that of National Socialism and apartheid. He writes:

> The global economic system, as the stronghold of huge agglomerations of power, is still the least recognised, the least exposed and answered challenge to the church to confess its faith. It is no longer amenable to control by any political institution for the good of all and at present costs the lives of over thirty million people annually, not to mention the human rights suppressed and violated in the interest of economic profit. (Duchrow, 1987)

For Duchrow, the global economic system is a 'confessional issue', which divides true Church from false Church. The idea derives from the 1934 Barmen Declaration, which argued that Christians faced a fundamental choice for or against Christ in the response they made to National Socialism. This cannot be a matter of words alone, but of concrete actions taken by both the Church and its members. To act as standard bearers for a new economic order is not merely an option for Christians, but the mark of what it is to be truly Church.

In this context, to adopt Investors is to be drawn yet further into the assumptions and practices of the global economic system. That system is idolatrous, in that it sets up a false god over and against Christ. Of course, the Church's stock market investments, its participation in capitalist exchange, and the unequal distribution of resources between churches across the world are equally wrong. But to engage with any late capitalist management mechanism is to make matters worse. On this reading, the details of Investors are largely irrelevant: the Church is challenged by its fundamental faith to a wholly different agenda.

2 *Investors represents the adoption of inappropriate managerialism*

This objection also places Investors in the context of the thinking that gave rise to it, but is more concerned with 'managerialism' than with the systemic nature of capitalism. It is possible to accept a broadly market economy, while still regarding modern big-business management as a degraded and exploitative manifestation of it. Noting the tendency of Anglican leaders to adopt the dominant ideology of their peer group, and the pervasiveness of managerial thinking in the public and private sectors, Richard Roberts writes:

> What is now new about the present situation of the Church of England is that the ideology of managerialism now being appropriated by its elite is infinitely more subtle and invasive than any of its clumsier predecessors. Indeed, the outstanding success of managerialism as an ideology (ie a comprehensive and regulatory system of interest-bearing ideas specifically incorporating the denial of the interest of its propagators) is that it fights off all-comers with the charge that resistance to the prerogatives and practices of managerial control is simply the expression of vested interests and an unwilling-ness to be efficient and accountable. The implementation of the latter invariably implies control. (Roberts, 1996)

Looked at in this way, Investors is a particularly subtle form of managerial control. The 'people' language disguises and makes palatable the selection and enforcement of management objectives. Training is designed to help people implement objectives that they may not subscribe to. The process of appraisal increases the capacity of management to dispense with those who challenge those objectives. Training and development are made entirely instrumental, rather than having their location in human flourishing. Investors thus carries the same authoritarian management assumptions as earlier top-down management, but packaged in such a way as to make people willing participants in the control exercised over them. Faced with this, the task of the Church is not to adopt Investors, but to challenge and expose its assumptions.

A less forthright approach admits the possibility that some forms of management are appropriate, but nevertheless points out that management techniques cannot be accepted as value-neutral. Stephen Pattison has argued that managerialism has many of the characteristics of religious faith. It uses language of commitment, identity, conversion and vision. The results of managerial action are often mixed, so it is carried ultimately by faith in an optimistic, forward-looking, instrumental pattern of belief and behaviour. Pattison is careful to argue for a dispassionate assessment of particular management techniques rather than their wholesale rejection. He nevertheless concludes:

> Part of the challenge of Christianity/religion to society is to promote a vision of human possibility, transcendence and mystery that stands over and against the closure and control represented by much management theory and practice. It will be sad, to say the least, if religious groups become unable to witness to anything other than the virtues of the managed, consumer-centred market place ostensibly focused on the perceived needs of religious 'customers'. (Pattison, 1997)

On this reading, Investors may have merit, and may even be beneficial in particular circumstances. However, for the Church to adopt it is to lose critical distance. It necessarily involves 'sanctifying' an aspect of modern managerialism that is also known in some circumstances to be exploitative and instrumental. The issue is not the balance of the strengths and weaknesses of Investors itself. It is the stance that Christianity takes to what has become the secular faith of managerialism. The Christian faith creates a presumption for critical evaluation, not for adoption.

3 Investors denies transcendent failure

This third objection deals more closely with the particular characteristics of Investors. It does not require the wholesale rejection of management techniques, let alone of the global economy. Rather, it focuses on the assumptions contained in the cycle of purpose, planning, action and evaluation. It is pointed out that Investors assumes a world of ordered and human-directed purposefulness; and takes for granted that it is open to human organizations to discern their purpose, make plans to achieve it, carry them out and, by an iterative process, bring the purpose to fruition. This is sometimes known as a 'success model'. But the world is not like that. It is unpredictable, chaotic and often impenetrable. Plans go wrong, purpose remains elusive, and evaluation often fails to reveal true causality.

This perspective finds support in management studies. In one of the best-regarded modern books on business strategy, John Kay notes that strategic planning failed to live up to expectations, and has gone out of fashion in many firms. He writes:

> Attempts to forecast the evolution of a firm more than a short period ahead are fundamentally useless. Two decades ago it seemed possible to believe that technology would ultimately conquer these problems. With sufficient information, and infinitely powerful computers, the uncertainties of business behaviour would gradually be resolved. We now know that this will never be true. Like the weather, business is a chaotic system in which small differences in the starting point can translate into large divergences in final outcomes. (Kay, 1993)

The Investors model represents 'best practice' in the late 1980s and 90s, and reflects the management consensus of the last decade. Thinking has moved on, and it is inevitable that a widely available model should lag behind leading-edge thinking. Reflecting on the failure of rationalist planning forced management thinkers to take more seriously aspects of human existence that had proved immune to it. A key element of this is the complex relationship between order and chaos, success and failure. Christianity proclaims a creator God who brought order out of chaos (Genesis 1.2). It also has a great deal to say about the nature of perceived failure.

The central focus of Christian faith is the cross. Our reconciliation to God was not made possible by anything that could be called successful in worldly terms, but by what seemed to be abject failure (1 Corinthians 1.23). In following Christ, we are asked to take up our cross (Luke 14.27; Matthew 10.38). St Paul is clear that worldly attributes and achievements are as nothing in relation to the value of knowing Christ (Philippians 3.8). By this he does not mean a theoretical knowledge, but the knowledge that comes from being caught up personally and totally in Christ's cross and resurrection.

God's relationship with Israel is an account of human failure repeatedly transformed by God's self-giving. Accounting for the fall of the northern kingdom, the Deuteronomist saw a pattern of failure to maintain the covenant which brought about the destruction of Israel (2 Kings 17.7). The perspective of the later prophets was that God's love transcended this failure, and would not be withdrawn (Isaiah 40.2). Indeed, it was by entering into human failure that God could re-establish the possibility of humankind being made in his own image.

Compared to this perspective, the 'success model' implied by Investors, it is argued, is frankly trivial. It requires the benefits of training to be recognized (Indicator 4.3), but makes no allowance for disbenefits. It talks about management competences, but makes no reference to management weaknesses. The possibility of failure makes no appearance. It is this that leads Stephen Pattison to argue that modern managerialism has the characteristics of a Christian heresy. It picks up the optimism derived from the hope that God will redeem humanity made in his image, but ignores the counter-balancing ideas of our sin, our limitations and our need for forgiveness.

However, many people have questioned whether Investors should be understood in this way. Bishop Jim Thompson has made the valuable point that to ask if something has gone well or badly does not imply a 'success model'. It is what we do with the answer that matters, and particularly how we handle failure. To resist evaluation can be to resist facing up to failure. Investors requires us to say whether we achieved what we set out to do. Whether we understand that as success or failure in transcendent or even worldly terms, and what we then choose to do about it, is for us to determine.

4 Investors does not meet the real needs of the Church

This objection does not involve demonstrating that Investors is wrong, either in respect of its particular content, or in respect of the management thinking from which it derives. Rather, it claims that Investors is inappropriate to the nature of Church, and particularly to the challenges that the Church faces today. In some ways, this is not a theological but a pragmatic objection. If there are tools more effective than Investors, it makes sense to use them. But the objection is not made on those grounds. Rather it is based on a particular interpretation of the dependency of the Church on the action of the Holy Spirit, a dependency taken to exclude reliance on secular management techniques.

The survey conducted in Ripon to establish clergy and lay attitudes to Investors sought responses to a number of statements about the Church and its future. The level of agreement to two statements is particularly striking: 58 per cent of clergy and 48 per cent of laity agreed strongly or very strongly that 'the Church must change radically to meet modern needs'; only 20 per cent of clergy and 29 per cent of laity agreed strongly or very strongly that 'the Church has much to learn from secular management'. Other questions revealed that 48 per cent of clergy agreed strongly or very strongly that there were too many diocesan initiatives, that only 18 per cent agreed strongly or very strongly that their PCC was willing to embrace change, but that 56 per cent agreed strongly or very strongly that the Church could embrace numerical decline, and that 65 per cent agreed strongly or very strongly that they were personally willing to embrace change.

If radical change is needed and welcomed by clergy, and it is not coming from PCCs, diocesan initiatives or secular management, where is it coming from? This question was not probed in the survey. It is difficult to find an answer in literature on Church growth, most of which makes explicit use of management insights. A clue is given by Christopher Moody's reflection on the concern he experienced as a chaplain at being asked to take on a counselling role:

> In the course of thinking things through I did indeed come to feel that my understanding of the pastoral task had become too detached from its roots in the belief that God is dynamically at work, immanently and redemptively, in his own creation, towards a final fulfilment. It is our privilege as pastors, co-workers and people of God, to discern this activity in whatever situation we are called and, in some way, to release and embody it in our own lives. To return to these roots means, I believe, to discard many of the notions about professional pastoral ministry which have helped to imprison this activity within church congregations, and to reach back to a different understanding of it as something authenticated on the basis of shared faith rather than claims to a particular professional competence and status. (Moody, 1992)

Moody assumes that there is an either/or choice between professional competences and a reliance on the dynamic work of God. Speaking of this dualism, the Anglican priest and anthropologist Paul Yates has written:

> Part of the antipathy to a humanly animated social realm is the question of the role of God as social actor or influence. The idea of people constructing their reality is seen as incompatible with a socially active divine planner. Who is in control? This theory implies a correspondence theory of language, that our words need to address a unified set of objects. As I have suggested, seamless reality may be posited and at the same time more than one voice may be heard addressing it, and not necessarily in unison. (Yates, 1998)

The Task Group believes that the seamless reality of creation can indeed be addressed in both theistic and secular language, without reducing one to the other or compromising the integrity of either. Nevertheless, the view that sociological analysis, professional competences and management techniques are competitive to dependency on God is deeply held. It is the most widespread objection to Investors to be found in the Church, and one that itself needs the most careful theological evaluation.

Understanding the objections

It would be possible to go through each of these objections and identify counter-arguments. To do so would be to sell short a point developed in Chapter 4: that participation in Investors enables the Church to engage fully in discussions about the human possibilities of modern organizations. For the Church to do this, it needs to be fully alive to the shadow side of Investors. A theological perspective which did not draw attention to Investors' capacity to side-step structural inequality, to be managerially coercive, to underestimate failure and to obscure the action of God in the world would have succumbed to prevailing managerial fashion. It would have lost its transformative capacity.

However, a general point must be made about objections based on what might be called 'guilt by association'. Anthony Thiselton has drawn attention to the subversive impact that the practice of reducing all statements to disguised power bids has, not just on disinterested and rational thought, but on the possibility of believing in a God of love. Is that, as Nietzsche argued, simply deception and manipulation exercised in the interests of the Church? Thiselton writes:

> It becomes arguable that a life based wholly on a hermeneutic of suspicion and iconoclasm has about it more than an element of self-contradiction. Granted that many bureaucrats live only to build empires, that many professional people put the interests of their guild before those of the public, or that many religious people treat religion and 'God' as a means of self-affirmation or for the purposes of power, by what doctrine (when the postmodern self rejects doctrine) can we say that all bureaucrats, professionals, or religious people live in this way? (Thiselton, 1995)

Taking the objections overall, the question is not whether they have merit, but whether they outweigh the positive case that can be made for Investors. To practise theology in this way is to allow the possibility of two perspectives to be held in tension. The practical experience of Investors was, in the main, productive, empowering and effective. Saying that is not to deny the validity of experiences of Investors as banal, coercive or time-wasting. A balanced judgement takes both types of experience into account.

Towards a balanced view

How does one weigh up the case for Investors and the objections that have been made to it? The case for is essentially that using Investors enables the Church in its present situation to come nearer to what God is calling it to be. The objection is essentially that Investors draws the Church away from God, towards a secular and alien paradigm.

The Dean of Lichfield, Tom Wright, is very clear in his perspective: 'If for one moment I thought Investors was taking us away from God, I would abandon it immediately.' The experience of Phil Williams, Vicar of St Barnabas, was that 'It was God and the people who did it. Investors was a channel; it was not the substance.' We believe these judgements are right, and that Investors can be commended to the Church on theological grounds. However, a caveat must be sounded which takes account of the objections, and which goes further even than Investors in providing the grounds for constructive theological engagement with modern organizational practice.

The Australian Anglican theologian, Kevin Giles, concludes an exhaustive study of the biblical grounds of the Church by reflecting on the relationship between the secular and sacred. He writes of the New Testament authors:

> Implicitly they all accept that the church is both a theological reality and a social reality. There are always these two aspects of the church; one cannot exist without the other. Indeed, Luke and Paul would suggest that the latter is needed for the former to thrive. The problem of too much structuring and too little interest in the dynamic work of the Holy Spirit, a problem ever since the apostolic age, is not an issue for them. Yet just as they affirm the importance of institutional form, they also lay down the principle that there should always be a controlling force – namely, the freedom of the Holy Spirit to renew the church by raising up Spirit-filled leaders who will call the Christian community back to its roots. (Giles, 1995)

The challenge we face is to be sufficiently sure of God's gracious gift, and of the sustaining work of the Holy Spirit, to engage positively and confidently with the organizational patterns offered by modern society. We do so not in the vain hope that those patterns are complete in themselves, but in the knowledge that their inevitable failures are forgiven by God if (and only if) our focus is on living out his purpose through their use. In that context, and by both its internal logic and the results that it brings, we believe that Investors can be judged to be appropriate for use by the Church.

4

Needs and Challenges
Facing the Church

How can Investors help the Church? In this chapter we explore some of the needs and challenges which face the contemporary Church and then assess how Investors can help to meet them. Some challenges are external and concern the nature of the modern world. So, in recent years, developing a vision and strategic planning have become important tools for churches working out a missionary response to new cultural situations and changing worldviews. Other challenges arise from the internal structures of the Church's own organization and from its difficulty in translating its vision into practice. As one diocesan bishop put it: 'I know there is a hole but I don't know how to fill it.'

It is our view that dioceses and parishes often don't see how to express their visionary purpose in practical concrete ways. We argue that Investors can offer a framework which would enable the Church to develop a clearer understanding of its mission; and identify concrete ways of fulfilling it, with the constituent parts relating more effectively to the whole.

Responses to a changing world

However one interprets the figures, there has been a major decline in patterns of churchgoing ever since the height of attendance in the Victorian period. The downward trend has increased even more rapidly since the 1960s, with steady reductions in the numbers of people coming forward for baptism and confirmation, in attendance at services, and in just about every other index (Currie *et al.*, 1977). There is, of course, considerable local variation. Some churches, particularly those in evangelical and charismatic traditions, are more effective in holding on to their children and young people. It is also true that patterns of church attendance have changed. Many people do not go to church every Sunday but, as a survey in the Ripon Diocese has identified, do go on other days or less than every week. Samples taken on one day do not therefore give a reliable figure for total church attendance. There is, nevertheless, a more widespread concern that faith and churchgoing are no longer viewed as important in Britain and that churches have little impact on the larger part of the population (Greenwood, 1988; Warren, 1995). It does seem that there is a continuing interest in issues of spirituality, but little interest in membership of a religious organization. Grace Davie has characterized the situation in British society faced by the churches, but also by other traditional institutions, as that of 'believing but not belonging' (Davie, 1994).

Explanations of and responses to this decline vary. At heart, the issue is the Church's continuing need to respond to new cultural situations and rapidly changing social patterns. These are now characterized by the proliferation of meanings, as well as new patterns of work, technology, family, community life and communications, which can be seen as leading to crises of faith and meaning. The new contexts and challenges have been well described in the Board of Education Report *Tomorrow is Another Country* (1996) and also in the Board of Mission Report *The Search for Faith and the Witness of the Church* (1996).

Robin Gill sees these as theological issues as well as strategic ones (Gill, 1988). He argues for a 'praxis theology', which requires theologians not only to be concerned with ideas but also to give attention to the structures which support, flow from and even challenge these ideas. Focusing on worship, clergy deployment and patterns of ministry in rural and urban communities, Gill is convinced that 'established patterns do need to be challenged. The temptation for declining churches is to stick to what is already established rather than to embark upon risky change.'

In our survey of Ripon Diocese we asked what people saw as the most important task facing the Church today. Many responses referred to the need to be more effective in relating the Christian tradition to life as it is actually being lived and experienced now. For example, one respondent says:

> The Church must get involved with real life and see that it is part of life. It must be professional, receptive, and respectful of the congregation – style must be modified so that the Church becomes a leader and less didactic. The Church must get real!

We suggest that there are three fundamental questions. Is Christian faith tenable in conditions of modernity and postmodernity? If so, is it sustainable without belonging to a community or network of believers? If not, what structures of sustainability are desirable and feasible?

Our view is that Christian faith is both tenable and necessary in contemporary society. It is not the place of this report to go into these issues, but we note that the arguments of, for example, the secularization thesis, for the sustained erosion of religious faith in the modern world, are not borne out in actual experience. There is a continued and growing interest in matters of faith and spirituality, as the proliferation of 'spirituality' sites on the Internet bears witness. Even those, such as in the Sea of Faith, who construe faith as a human creation are at least concerned with the centrality of faith in human life. The work of people like John Polkinghorne has demonstrated how the contemporary, science-dominated world is not inimical to religious believing.

But is believing sustainable without structures of belonging? Our view is that, unless we address these issues, in the future there may be neither belonging nor believing. In other words, people need to see the possibilities of faith by seeing it credibly practised. Although faith is not a product in the commercial sense, one member of our Task Group pointed up the following interesting analogy related to marketing. With the rise of television and video, it was assumed that the age of the cinema was over. But cinema re-conceptualized its product and, in fact, cinema going is on the increase and new multi-complexes are opening each week. Our view is that there is similarly a need for the Church to re-conceptualize what it offers, to maximize the number and types of opportunities where faith might be shared and the gospel heard. We do not need to lie down in the face of a determinist sociology, but must develop many different styles of being Church, and of living and giving expression to the Christian faith.

It is not our task to spell out what the new structures might be. Our view is that they will vary according to different needs and contexts. We believe that Investors is one helpful process which encourages the Church, at different levels, to explore how it might proclaim the gospel afresh in the circumstances in which it is placed, or to which it feels called.

Strategic responses to date

Strategic thinking in the Church is not new. Responses from diocesan secretaries describe the kind of 'vision and planning' initiatives that dioceses have undertaken. These have addressed such issues as:

- the needs of the local community;

- the nature of ministry and ministerial provision;

- the role of diocesan structures including that of senior staff;

- the deployment of lay and ordained specialist advisers;

- the re-structuring and composition of boards and councils;

- schemes for staff appraisal;

- the ever-present concerns about financial viability.

There have been concerns about the reactive rather than proactive nature of the Church's strategy, which leads, for example, to inefficiency and the weariness of moving from project to project with no evaluation and no prioritizing of objectives. Some dioceses have tried to address the problem, also shared by the national Church, of the confusions between the episcopal, synodical, resourcing and service systems (Turnbull Report, 1995). Often this has led to structural changes, such as the devolution of some power to deaneries or the restructuring of boards and councils. The rationale behind these developments has been to improve the effectiveness and efficiency of the Church and to be led by the demands of ministry and mission and not by finance. A variety of approaches have been used, such as reviews, mission statements, planning targets, mission audits, strategy statements and so forth.

A detailed and unpublished survey of dioceses conducted by David Lane of the Diocese of Southwell shows how dioceses have been undertaking a wave of reviews during the 1990s, all in response to exactly the same internal factors (perceived poor communication, top-heavy structures) and external factors (declining numbers and finance). The survey indicates a picture of fragmentation, of separate units each struggling to work out in isolation its own answer to similar questions, to re-invent the wheel. His conclusions are that:

- The entry points into the reviews have been different – some dioceses starting with major audits, some with mission statements, some with reviews of specific aspects of structure. This creates an appearance of diversity that is greater than it actually is, because it is only a diversity of sequence.

- The dioceses have ended up over time with much the same cluster of solutions: mission statements, parish audits, merging DBF and synod, fewer committees, devolution to deaneries, more lay training.

- There remain some areas where no consensus has emerged, and where practice is divergent. Of these the most important is the assessment of quota. This is critical because financial arrangements expose real relationships.

- All dioceses reveal unresolved questions of linkage between tiers (parish, deanery, diocese), linkage between forms of authority (synodical, episcopal, professional), and linkage between processes (training, planning, budgeting).

- There is very little use of evaluation and benchmarking.

Often clergy experience initiatives like these reviews as part of the problem rather than a solution. In rural and urban parishes everywhere, clergy speak of increasing pressures caused by such things as:

- making sense of and communicating faith in a secular culture;

- the effect of changing patterns of church attendance;

- the problem of historic or obsolete buildings;

- increasing workloads caused by fewer clergy and amalgamating parishes;

- preference for more traditional 'solo' styles of working;

- poor systems of support;

- higher expectations of lay people;

- higher maintenance costs with pressure on incomes;

- steadily increasing parish shares.

So much of the work of the clergy seems to be about running a profitable local church, rather than carrying out the ministerial or priestly functions for which they believe they were ordained. To clergy under such pressures, diocesan or bishops' strategies can seem a hindrance. Without clergy support, important initiatives frequently fail to achieve any significant and lasting change. Those that are supported but then not followed up create considerable weariness and cynicism: although a lot of work was put in, 'nothing came of it'. Clergy and lay leaders can easily become cynical about the latest bright idea from the diocese, and the polarization between 'us' and 'them' is exacerbated.

So why have these initiatives not achieved what they set out to do? We identify three main reasons: inadequate models of ministry, poor implementation and antipathy to 'management'.

Inadequate models of ministry

Bishops and clergy commonly describe their experience of ministry in terms of loneliness. This is partly to do with the nature of any kind of responsibility and the knowledge that 'the buck stops here'. But in the Church it is also to do with the pervasiveness of solo ministry. It is not uncommon to hear clergy speaking of 'my vision' for the parish, or of the changes that they plan to make in 'my' new parish. Often lay readers say that they do not feel they are utilized as fully as they could be. Lay people who have undertaken training frequently express disappointment that they are not encouraged to develop their skills in the parish. In the Diocese of Bangor, senior clergy who met for a two-day training session on Investors warmly expressed their appreciation that they were doing such an exercise, for the first time, 'with their bishop among them'.

The idea of the lone chief on top of the pyramid is abnormal and deeply un-Christian. No-one can be perfect alone, and we all need the support and correcting influence of close colleagues. Robert Greenleaf argues that a self-protective image of omniscience often evolves from the warped and filtered communications which result from pyramidal structures because of the way these weaken informal links and dry up channels of honest reaction. The effect is to distort the leader's judgement, best sharpened through interaction with others who are free to challenge and criticize. Persons atop pyramids are usually very alone; they are not on the grapevine. It is assumed, says Greenleaf, that one-person-in-control leads to decisiveness where it is needed. In fact, the result is often indecisiveness and at great cost to the organization. We often complain that there are too few leaders, but with pyramidal structures only a few can emerge, and these are always overburdened.

There is a counter-movement from those in the Church who believe that all are called, that all share in the common priesthood of the Church and that ministry and discipleship are tasks of the whole people of God. There is increasing interest in and experiment with new forms of ministry variously called 'local ministry', 'shared', 'collaborative', 'team ministry', 'total ministry' and so forth. Sometimes these are informal arrangements, and sometimes they are formalized into legal teams. These new expressions, with their different shapes, can be a way of maintaining traditional structures, of helping out the hard-pressed clergy; but they may also represent new possibilities of engagement with God's mission in a pluralistic world.

They also imply demands for new forms of training in collaborative styles of ministry, both in theological colleges and in non-residential programmes of ministry training for lay and ordained. Two consultations

organized by the Edward King Institute propose that new learning opportunities must now include training in: tackling change creatively, building
vision, dealing with conflict, forms of power-sharing and mutuality, part-
nerships with the wider community, as well as developing a culture of
continuous reflection and learning. The point here is that these are new
skills for the Church and its leaders.

The approach of much contemporary management theory and practice is
towards subsidiarity, and yet many bishops and clergy are reluctant to
share power and accept structures of joint accountability with leadership
teams and through different levels in the organization. In diocesan structures there is often a withholding of information, which retains power but
hinders proper collaboration. As a diocesan adviser succinctly put it: 'We
have a policy of collaborative ministry in this diocese but very little actual
collaboration.' Underlying all this is a fundamental issue of trust. The
Church must give room for people to grow and to be trusted to take shared
responsibility as part of the common priesthood.

Resources and implementation

The review of the first half of the Decade of Evangelism made the chal-
lenging point that:

> Though 're-structuring for mission' is virtually always now
> identified as the goal of re-structuring, retrenchment is
> sometimes what is actually being managed. Perhaps the key
> test of this distinction is the identification as to where
> resources are being released to forward mission. If no
> resources are being put into development then only
> retrenchment is happening. (Warren, 1996)

Re-deployment of resources is not the only issue. The problem is also that
often little or no attention is given to how a plan is to be implemented.
Grand visions are generated, bold policies are created, but no-one
addresses the tasks of implementation. We may have the grand aim, for
example, of showing God's love for the people of our parish or conurbation,
but people need to know what precisely they should do today! The task is
how to translate the big vision into achievable goals and without
paralysing people with unrealistic aims. The question is not only about
vision, or even about how we bring it in, but about how we make it work.

Experience from management consultancy suggests that lack of attention
to the pathways of implementation is not only a shortcoming of the
Church:

Organizations traditionally emphasise the determination of a strategy for gaining distinctive competitive advantage in the market place, but few explicitly address the cultural and leadership path required to realise such a strategy. (Schneider, 1997)

By 'cultural', Schneider is referring to all that makes up an organization's method of operation, how it achieves its goals. It is everything to do with implementation. Schneider quotes research suggesting that culture is so critical to visionary organization that its leaders should focus on building the organization per se rather than on doing the business of the organization. This is so important that:

The essence of a visionary company comes in the translation of its core ideology and its own unique drive for progress into the very fabric of the organization – into goals, strategies, tactics, policies, processes, cultural practices, management behaviour, building layouts, pay systems, accounting systems, job design – into everything that the company does. (Collins and Porras, 1994)

This emphasis on the importance of implementation is closely related to current thinking on learning organizations (Senge, 1994). Learning organizations are those that are open to their environment, purposeful, aligned and continually reflecting and evaluating (Warren, 1998). 'Alignment' here refers to congruence between principles and practice – all the elements of the organization working in harmony with its core ideology and the goals it wishes to achieve.

So, in growing numbers of dioceses, the most laudable plans are initiated to further the Kingdom, share resources, or develop collaborative ministry – which in fact change very little because fundamental 'how' questions are not addressed and because sufficient resources are not put into implementation. This explains why so often clergy and lay leaders become weary and cynical of 'yet another initiative'. Successful organizations, on the other hand, are ones that, over time, 'have a clear strategy, a leadership approach that consistently mobilises people to understand and accomplish that strategy and understand and build and live out the culture that most effectively fits the strategy' (Schneider, 1997). In other words, the strategy has to be energizing and practical, and translated into every aspect of the fabric of the organization's life and culture through the encouragement and mobilization of its entire people.

Antipathy to 'management'

Investors in People, or any other strategic tool, will need to overcome some antipathy in the Church towards 'management'. We have addressed the theological issues surrounding this in Chapter 3, but it is worth noting here that this is not an issue for the Church alone. Scepticism towards management is a common feature of values-led organizations. Landry and others argue that a neglect or mistrust of management is endemic in voluntary and non-profit organizations (Landry et al., 1992). They suggest that people in such organizations tend to be more enthusiastic about the direct work of the organization and antipathetic towards 'administration'. Professional staff are often at pains to avoid what they see as 'interference' in their work. This analysis is supported by Handy, who makes the point that voluntary organizations often like to emphasize the 'voluntary' and play down the 'organization' (Handy, 1988). In their classic work on the self-righteous ineptitude of some community-based organizations, Landry et al. make the point that:

> The wholesale rejection of management theory, as part of capitalist ideology, has had the unfortunate effect of throwing the baby out with the bath water. This perspective fails to disentangle the role of management as a necessary administrative function within any organization, regardless of its political purposes, from the particular 'command structure' form of management which has developed in traditional business organizations. (Landry et al., 1985)

This is a view shared by Raymond Williams, a committed and revered socialist. He described 'management' as a slippery word but, in an essay on the Miners' Strike, he argues:

> there is, of course, virtually everywhere, a need for genuine management. Research, organization and planning are crucial in every complex organization. What is false in the currently imposed meanings of management is the reduction of these necessary processes to elements of the corporate plan of an employer looking only, in his own terms, to his version of profitable operation. (Williams, 1989)

Williams identifies a 'genuine management' which he sees as a demanding process including the continuous and complex exchange of information, negotiation of meaning, and the making of general and negotiated plans and agreements. Management can therefore be seen as a crucial function involving the clarification of an organization's goals and the continuous development and monitoring of the policies and procedures to implement them.

> The problem – how to clarify objectives, create a strategy to carry them out and find the means to make them happen, is one that few radical organizations recognise explicitly – most just muddle through. (Landry *et al.*, 1992)

It is difficult to avoid the conclusion that churches, too, are often content simply to muddle through.

The need for a framework

The Church may not have adequate models of itself as an organization. The images of 'family' or 'community' are still commonly used. These, of course, have good biblical foundation and describe the commitment and belonging that are proper to life in the Body of Christ. In reality, the Church is a very complex organization functioning at many different levels. The fact that 'the diocese' is often made into the villain may be explained as an attempt to split off part of this complexity. The saying of many promoted clerics, 'I am really a parish priest at heart', may reflect a flight from the more complex realities of organizational life and a failure to manage themselves in role.

Morgan describes how the metaphors or images we use for an organization can throw light on the way we think about and behave towards it. For instance, we may think of an organization as a machine, or as an organism or a body. What such images cannot do is spell out the kind of structure that the organization then requires. Images such as 'body' or 'vine', for example, do not tell us about the kind of structure that the Church needs on a day-to-day basis. This has to be developed out of the image. To fulfil the purposes expressed by the image, an organization needs an operational framework.

Some of the language of 'family' and 'community' rightly protests against the deadening features of bureaucracy but, if the Church of England is to be more than a set of local, largely independent congregations, then we have to address organizational issues. We have to do some joined-up thinking about the interrelationships and interdependence of the Church at its different levels – parish, deanery, cathedral, diocese, national and global. Because of the demands of mission as well as resources for mission, parishes can no longer afford to think of the diocese as 'them'.

We have to design more effective and properly managed Church organizations which enable us to operate simultaneously at more than one level.

How can Investors help the Church?

The Task Group has identified the following strengths of Investors:

● It is *mission-centred*

Perhaps the first step for any organization improving its effectiveness is to be clear about what kind of organization it is and what are its goals and purposes. For the Church, this means being clear about its purpose and mission. Investors helps an organization to state clearly its goals and purposes. (It has been suggested that this is the most critical task that confronts leaders.) For many people, the purpose of the Church may be obvious: for example, the proclamation of the gospel. However, there is still the important question of how this, or any other goal, is to be pursued in the present circumstances.

Moreover, it is not just a matter of clergy and lay leaders telling everyone what the goals are. There will need to be careful consultation if people are to be helped to understand their part and contribution as members of the Body of Christ. Investors requires a statement not only of the goals and targets but also of who will undertake them, what their support and training needs will be and how these will be met. Investors offers a way of taking seriously the idea that 'All Are Called'.

● It *builds on other work and is integrating and holistic*

Investors does not have to be 'yet another scheme', an additional burden on already hard-pressed clergy and laity. The advantage of Investors is that it can build on what is already happening. As has been mentioned in Chapter 1, it is not so much about 'doing' Investors as about making use of it. Many parishes will find that they are already along the road of what is required and that Investors both affirms and takes forward their work. For other parishes, Investors may offer a new framework for thinking about the nature of mission and ministry that has not yet been undertaken.

In our view, Investors, with its people-centred approach, may help to overcome both negative and uncritical attitudes to management. In Lenton Abbey, for example, as in other parishes in our survey, people commented on the way Investors had been a freeing process.

Investors offers a challenge to the Church to put into practice, in its own life and structures, its belief in a God who invests in people. Turnbull

(Archbishops' Commission, 1995) and Bridge (House of Bishops, 1997) stress the primacy of mission and identify people as the Church's greatest resource. Investors in People offers a framework by which God's people can establish their purpose, equip themselves and evaluate and review their contribution to the Missio Dei – this is a theological imperative.

Investors focuses on the experiences of all people in an organization. Success is judged by the experiences of everyone, at whatever level. So Investors helps organizations to value their members, by encouraging talent, developing individuals and working to ensure that common values and relationships are always maintained. Secular organizations, voluntary groups and churches have benefited from Investors, because it has led them to improve their clarity of purpose, value those involved and provide better support and training. Implementing Investors can be (but doesn't need to be) bureaucratic, imposed and costly in time and money. The Standard's value rests with those who interpret and seek to implement it and with their willingness to be honest, open and critical.

A number of people we have spoken to have pointed up the value of Investors in improving the morale of clergy and lay people. The focus on purpose, translation into achievable goals, and attention to training and support all have the effect of affirming people in their ministry and dis-cipleship. People have commented on the improved atmosphere in their church. This is important where people sometimes lack confidence in taking up roles in the local church. Investors can be an affirming process in which people feel valued. This is as important in diocesan structures as in parishes. Sometimes those who work in diocesan offices can be treated very cursorily or even rudely by people from parishes, whilst those who act as advisers can feel that they are always having to justify their role. Another word that people have used is 'belonging'. Enabling people to see how their contribution relates to the wider mission of the parish, diocese or department fosters a greater sense of belonging as well as purpose.

- **It provides opportunities for development, support and training**

Because it focuses on how people are prepared and supported for the roles they take up, Investors is good at identifying training needs and encouraging leaders to see how those needs may be met. Sometimes people are put off by the notion of training, perhaps by their more negative experiences of compulsory education. But most people respond to the idea of being supported and helped to do what they undertake.

Investors offers a way for clergy and leaders to listen to church members.

Taking seriously the fact that all the baptized are members of the Body and have a contribution to make involves more than the occasional 'Any comments?' It requires processes of encouragement, careful listening and ways of developing objectives, so that people feel they have been really heard. It involves the drafting and re-drafting of discussion documents, for example. 'This is what we think we heard you say. Tell us, have we got it right?' Investors involves a careful description of who is to be involved, and how they are to be consulted and supported in taking up their role.

This does not always require formal training programmes. More informal, in-house opportunities can be found to support and encourage people to develop their understanding and skills. In one diocese, effective work has gone on with PCC members, for example, many of whom had never had it explained what was actually required of them on a PCC. Parishes and deaneries which are identifying training and support needs in this way will be much better placed to shape the training provision in the diocese by requesting what they need.

There is a close identification in Investors between development and training. We think that this emphasis on development and support is right, and fits the situation in many parishes, which may discover that these things are already happening where people are being supported and encouraged.

- **It creates a culture of continuous learning**

As has already been discussed, some excellent schemes and ideas in the Church often flounder because not enough attention is given to implementation, to the 'how' as well as to the 'what' we do as a Church, whether in mission, social responsibility, worship or training. This explains what has been the main motive behind the adoption of Investors in People. In one diocese it was pressure from parishes and deaneries that led to the use of Investors as a process to find ways of carrying forward their concerns to improve their worship, the nurture and growth of members as disciples of Christ, and the relation of faith to the world around. Investors is effective in helping people translate the ongoing mission of the gospel into practical and achievable tasks. This is a process often missing from developing mission statements: people need to know how the grand aim is translated into practical and achievable steps. How does an aim such as 'Expressing God's love for this community', for example, translate into agreed goals that affect all the different groups and aspects of the life of the local church? Sometimes it may not involve doing anything additional, but doing some things differently and more effectively.

It is sometimes said that in the Church we have no means of evaluating what we do. We can only sow the seeds of possibility; the fruits cannot always be seen. There is some truth in this. How can you possibly measure people's increasing faith or spirituality? Increasing numbers are not necessarily a reliable measure of gospel commitment. That being said, there is a valid question about the Church learning from its experience, and this must involve some kind of criteria for success. This is obviously true at diocesan level. Dioceses have limited resources but unlimited possibilities for mission and ministry. So there are key questions about how those resources are to be used effectively and efficiently. How do we decide whether to continue to fund one particular activity as opposed to another? How do we decide whether one particular activity has served its purpose or should be continued? Sometimes dioceses have very imaginative schemes or programmes, but these are not always evaluated. Similarly, there are few opportunities for learning about best practice across parish, deanery and diocesan boundaries.

People come to church, or use the services and ministries offered, but we often have little idea about how these are valued or what could be done to improve them. It is felt that people are giving time and energy to these things and that is all we need to know. Investors encourages churches to look at what they do or plan to do, and to ask how they will know if they achieve what they set out to do. Building on what has been accomplished can be a very affirming and encouraging process. It is also good steward-ship and means that precious resources are not wasted on re-inventing wheels that fail.

Until recently the classic route for achieving the Investors Standard was by external assessment. Now there is the option of other routes making use of internal audits. Though some parishes dislike the notion of external assessment, others have commented on the value of someone from out-side coming to share plans and achievements. Some parishes also value the discipline that is imposed by having to prepare for an external asses-sor, and feel they would not have achieved all their preparation without this.

The fact that Investors is a widely used benchmark in private industry and in the public and voluntary sectors means that it can offer a way for the Church to assess its effectiveness alongside other organizations and groups. It is a practical way for the Church to demonstrate, in a commonly understood language, its commitment to people, their wellbeing and development. It is also a challenge to the Church: do you really practise what you preach?

The commitment of the members of our Technical Group has also shown how pleased lay people are to offer skills and insights from their occupations to the Church's life. This has shown them that the Church is willing to learn from best practices in the wider community and that they have something to contribute. As someone said, 'Investors engages with the real world, where people are.'

By using the common language offered by Investors, the Church itself also has an opportunity to contribute to wider debates. Many people are concerned about the threat posed to human values in some organizations by solely commercial objectives and instrumental criteria for success. By involvement in the Investors process, and in conversation with members of TECs and other advisers and consultants, the Church can bear witness to its values. The translation process is not only from Investors to the Church but also from the Church and what it has to offer to the Investors process. The Task Group has already made a contribution to a recent review of the Investors process. The Board of Education has also contributed to the Government's consultation document, *The Learning Age*, already referred to.

The development of collaboration

Essentially the task is not a question of selling Investors but of introducing different ways of thinking. How are people in this church involved fully in developing its life and mission and in its key decisions? How far do people feel that their gifts are affirmed and that they are able to contribute to the life of the gathered church and beyond it? What is being done to offer inclusive and stimulating learning opportunities and to encourage people to take them up? How far is learning a natural part of the church's life and people's experience of the church one of enrichment? How far and in what ways are we offering people a tangible spiritual experience? Are they receiving it? How do we know? These are the kind of questions that Investors is promoting. They go to the heart of the Church's purpose and ought to be part of every church's life.

5

A Structure for Investors in the Church

From the beginning of its work, the Task Group faced the question of 'levels'. The Church had committed to Investors as diocese, parish, cathedral and diocesan staff. Is it logical to commit at these different levels? If not, is one level more appropriate than another? Real questions are involved. If parishes are involved separately, will there be coherence between their plans and those of deanery and diocese? Can a diocesan staff truly be 'Investors' without considering its relationship to parishes? Can a parish be truly 'Investors' outside the diocesan family?

These questions hold a mirror to a Church which claims to be interdependent, to share ministry and oversight at several levels, and to operate on principles of subsidiarity, unity and diversity. They are primarily questions about what makes us more than a congregational church. They are about 'the whole and the parts'. Investors poses these questions because it wants organizations to be recognized as 'whole organizations', and not as fragmented parts that deny or evade their interdependence. There are three main reasons for avoiding a fragmented approach:

● It limits the benefits to the organization.

● It adds greatly to the cost of assessment.

● It causes confusion about the use of the Investors badge.

To be asked to consider our own 'wholeness' is an unexpected but theologically fruitful consequence of considering the Church's involvement with Investors. This chapter sets out considerations of unity and diversity in secular organizations and in the Church, the guidelines offered by IIPUK, and the Task Group's proposals for the Church of England.

Unity and diversity in large organizations

In the first seven years of the Investors Standard, large organizations have worked towards recognition in a variety of ways. At one extreme, organizations have used Investors to achieve consistency and simultaneous change across their whole operation. At the other extreme, organizations have allowed a particularly enthusiastic unit to commit and achieve recognition on its own, with little effect on the rest of the organization. Neither of these approaches is wholly satisfactory. Experience has shown that a number of factors must be taken into account.

- Going for Investors as a whole organization can be too bold a step to take in one go, particularly as people may be uncertain of the real benefits. So local piloting makes sense.

- Organizations increasingly want to encourage local initiative, and local responses to local needs, and a single national programme can stifle that.

- Conversely, having unnecessarily different procedures in different places causes confusion when staff change job, increases costs, and prevents the sharing of best practice.

- Going for recognition as an 'area' or at another intermediate level creates problems if boundaries then change. So it is important to be clear which boundaries will be long-standing.

Of course, all organizations are different. Some have a number of similar or 'clone' outlets with little local freedom. Others are groupings of almost wholly separate businesses. Organizations can also be moving in different directions at any particular time – some to greater unity, some to greater diversity. There can be no single approach for all organizations. Some practical examples illustrate the balance needed.

Marks and Spencer is a strongly centralized organization in many ways, not least in its culture. Store managers are now expected to use their local knowledge to develop their own business plans that reflect their particular marketplace. As in most retailing, store managers move about quite frequently. Marks and Spencer therefore evolved a strategy of local ownership of Investors in each store, involving all levels of staff. One objective is to ensure that practice is well embedded and will survive changes in local management.

A national charity had allowed so much local diversity that this was leading to variable standards of service, putting at risk both the charity's reputation with social services professionals and the good name on which it depended for donations. Its Investors programme was therefore more centrally directed, and had the aim of more consistent standards of service, identity and evaluation.

The NatWest Group took a third approach. Its main businesses – Corporate Banking, Retail Banking and Mortgage Services – implemented the Standard and achieved recognition each in their own right. They were clearly separate businesses within the NatWest 'family'. The Group had two main central offices, for NatWest Retail and NatWest Group. They needed separately tailored approaches, but were still one 'head office'. So they developed two implementation plans, but had a single assessment.

In all these cases, organizations are finding the particular combination of unity and diversity that best enables them to fulfil their own purposes within their own cultural traditions and in accordance with their own objectives. Investors does not impose a single model of 'wholeness'. It does oblige organizations to think through what it means for them in practical terms.

Unity and diversity in the Church

The Church of England presents particular issues of unity and diversity. They are unique to the Church in the same way as those of any large organization are unique. They are by the same measure analogous to those of other large organizations. In particular, 'wholeness' must address:

- the operation of some functions, such as the selection of ordination candidates, at a national level;

- the rights of PCCs and incumbents, entrenched at local level;

- the principle that bishop and incumbent share the cure of souls;

- the significant organizational role of dioceses;

- the balance of episcopal and synodical authority in the Church;

- the participation of the Church in the world-wide Anglican Communion;

- the Church's relationship to the state;

- the existence of separate jurisdictions, such as the Royal Peculiars.

It is possible to look at the structures of the Church of England and conclude that they are incapable of rational analysis. One diocesan secretary told us: 'The whole point of the structures is to stop people doing anything.' But to leave the matter there would be to evade our responsibility to discover the 'wholeness' encapsulated in the four marks of the Church: that it is one, holy, catholic and apostolic. The recent Turnbull and Bridge

Reports have sought to address this by examining in turn the central structures of the Church and the operation of synodical government. They have
been paralleled by reviews in the majority of dioceses of diocesan structure. They have in common a primary focus on structure. They have not
engaged primarily with how structures are used – the culture, the plans,
the style and the behaviour that bring structures to life. Everyone knows
that you can have diocesan synods with identical constitutions that are
totally dissimilar in how they 'really work'. In developing a structure for
Investors in the Church, we have had particular regard to how the Church
'really works' and the steps that can be taken to make it work better.

Investors guidelines

'Authority and autonomy' are the technical terms used by Investors in
People UK to determine which levels or parts of a complex organization
have the authority to make the decision to commit to working towards the
Standard, and which levels or parts are sufficiently autonomous to be
regarded as 'whole' organizations. IIPUK provides guidelines about this,
but it is for advisers, assessors and recognition panels, using the guidelines as support, to judge each application. In this respect, the practice of
IIPUK parallels the idea of dispersed and interdependent authority that is
a characteristic of Anglicanism.

Until September 1997, the guidelines were highly specific. Now they reflect
an understanding of dispersed authority and interdependence which is
entirely compatible with thinking in the Church.

They recognize that organizations 'want to work with the Standard in ways
that best suit their structure and culture'. Organizations are encouraged to
have an overall plan for all sub-units to work with the Standard. This will
often mean identifying the most appropriate 'building-blocks' within the
organization, which will then work towards recognition at their own speed.
The guidelines recognize that an overall plan will not be possible in all
cases, and recommend continuing dialogue between the organization and
the Investors network so that other parts of the organization can be added
as and when they are ready. The guidelines nevertheless maintain the
principle that the whole organization is the level at which the full benefits
of Investors are to be experienced.

The Task Group believes that these guidelines go with the grain of the
Church of England. Engaging with them will help us address the question
of how we express our relatedness in practical terms.

General Synod support

The Task Group is pleased that General Synod will be asked to receive this report as part of a debate on 'A Learning Church for a Learning Age' and at the same time as it is asked to receive the report of the Working Party on Lay Discipleship. We believe these two initiatives are key components of a vital need to promote lifelong learning and to develop a learning Church.

This is an appropriate time to be thinking of a learning Church. National initiatives regarding the development of 'the Learning Age' and initiatives in the Church point the same way. In his Pastoral Letter to clergy and people of the Anglican Communion following Lambeth 1998, the Archbishop of Canterbury wrote:

> We know that we must ensure that our structures are more accountable; we know that we must find ways of supporting the poorest parts of the Communion (often rich in faith and joy); we know that we must become a more outward-looking and serving Communion; we know that we must share together our resources in training and biblical scholarship.

Accountable and interdependent structures, an outward-looking and serving people, and shared training resources are all marks of a learning Church. We hope that General Synod will give unanimous endorsement to our proposals for the use of the Investors process as a means of development and training for mission. At a national level, the Church exercises authority through the House of Bishops, the General Synod and the Archbishops' Council. It therefore falls to the General Synod to commend Investors to dioceses, to set out the Standard's relationship to the Church's mission and development, and to agree the policy framework for its implementation. We also hope that, in due course, the central structures of the Church will embrace Investors as a tool to help in the major restructuring that the implementation of Turnbull entails. However, it would be inappropriate and impractical for there to be a single, national programme to implement Investors in the Church of England. We are simply not a centralized church.

The diocese is the appropriate unit

Anglican ecclesiology leads us to regard the diocese as the fundamental 'building-block' for Investors in the Church of England. We recommend this for the following reasons:

- The Church is called to order its life and work within the understanding of God's mission and does so through a complex, balanced and adaptive process of dispersed authority.

- Bishops and synods, clergy and laity at national, provincial, diocesan deanery and parish levels share this authority.

- No single unit can disregard the balance of subsidiarity and mutuality.

- No single level can claim authority or autonomy unequivocally.

- The primary Anglican organizational concept is the bishop in synod.

- The cure of souls is shared between bishop and incumbent, making the bishop present in every parish.

- It is at diocesan level that the full range of administrative, training, mission and support mechanisms can be found.

It is the principle of the shared cure of souls that leads us to regard the parish as less than ideal as the fundamental building-block for Investors in the Church. A parish can (and should) set out its own plans, and have its own identity, accounts and training budget. It can therefore meet the technical criteria set by IIPUK for 'authority and autonomy'. But this is to neglect the fact that its ministry is always exercised in communion with, and under the oversight of, its bishop.

We also recognize that not all dioceses will feel able at this point to agree to a diocesan programme to achieve the Investors Standard. For this reason, we recommend two alternative models for consideration by dioceses.

Arrangements within the diocese

Common to both models is the recommendation that dioceses should, through their Bishop's Council, consider the appropriateness of Investors in the light of their particular situation.

MODEL A: A DIOCESAN PLAN

Under this model, the diocese adopts a plan to achieve Investors as a whole diocese. To do so may involve inviting particular parishes to act as pathfinders, and perhaps a particular deanery to pilot the process for the rest of the diocese. A diocesan plan need not be for simultaneous action across the diocese. It need not be described as 'Investors', but may use the name of an existing diocesan initiative. It may also start with the diocesan office, rather than with parishes. The point is that there is some overall plan and framework at diocesan level.

MODEL B: DIOCESAN APPROVAL

Under this model, the diocese gives general approval for parishes and other units to engage with Investors under the normal pastoral oversight of the bishop. This model may be adopted where, for example, it is felt appropriate to allow individual parishes and other units to develop local experience prior to deciding whether to adopt a plan for the diocese as a whole. It is, of course, possible for parishes to engage with Investors without diocesan approval. However, it is consistent with the principles of 'wholeness' on which this chapter is based that general approval and support should be sought and given.

CATHEDRALS AND COMPANIES LIMITED BY GUARANTEE

Cathedrals play a distinctive part in the life of the diocese, and are often major employers. There are arguments for cathedrals engaging with Investors in their own right. There are also arguments for them doing so as part of a wider diocesan commitment. We believe that this should be a matter for local decision.

There are bodies in dioceses which have a separate legal existence – for example, the Board of Finance or (in some dioceses) the Board of Social Responsibility. Where possible, we believe units should approach Investors as part of the diocesan family. However, there will be circumstances where particular units, such as a social services operation, are clearly distinct in identity, financing and objectives. Where to draw the line is, we believe, a matter for dioceses to decide.

EXPERIENCE AT PARISH LEVEL

Whichever of the above models is chosen, the experience of using Investors at parish level will be very similar. It has been said that the diocese is the fundamental unit for organization, the parish the fundamental unit for mission. It is at parish level that mission objectives will be set, the training needs of the great majority of laity determined, and most learning will take place. Under Model A, those responsible for setting plans will need to engage consciously with diocesan and deanery plans. Under Model B, they cannot ignore them: the diocese will still have plans and training resources that the parish will need to take into account. To describe Model A as 'centralized' and Model B as 'decentralized' is thus misleading. Model A requires explicit engagement with the interdependence that is a fact of diocesan life. Its capacity to make that interdependence work better than it currently does is the reason for the Task Group regarding it as the preferred model.

Model A also offers major benefits in terms of recognition. Gaining the Investors badge is never a sufficient reason for engaging with Investors. However, it is wise for dioceses to consider how those who do engage with Investors can be recognized for their achievements. It is for this reason that we propose the creation of a 'Bishop's Award'.

THE BISHOP'S AWARD

Universities have grappled with analogous issues of unity and diversity. Is it sensible for a particular department to be recognized separately from the university as a whole? Is it sensible for very different departments to operate on a single model? To answer this dilemma, a member of our Technical Group, Bob Thackwray, evolved a system in the University of Loughborough that is now being generalized across the higher education sector. The system is that:

- The university makes an overall commitment.

- Departments proceed towards Investors at their own pace.

- When they feel ready, departments apply for an internal review that mirrors an Investors assessment and recognition.

- When all departments have reached the Standard, the university as a whole applies for external recognition.

We believe that this model has much to recommend it. Parishes and other units in the diocese will start at different levels and need different timescales before they are ready for assessment. It is right for achievement to be recognized, and recognized within the family of the diocese. It is also right that the diocese is seen externally as the fundamental building-block. We therefore propose the following two-stage process for the dioceses which chose to follow Model A.

Parishes or units that feel ready for assessment would make arrangements for a review of quality in ministry and training in association with Investors in People. This would be made by a qualified assessor who would make a recommendation to a panel in the diocese that would include the bishop or his representative and a representative of the local TEC. It would also be possible for parishes or units to be assessed externally at this stage if they so wished.

Under recent changes the assessor from the local TEC would discuss with the diocese at the outset how it would like to be assessed. Then, when the diocese as a whole was ready to meet the Standard, the assessor would make a decision as to its readiness for recognition. Recognition that the diocese had achieved the Investors Standard would come from Investors' Assessment and Recognition Units or Recognition Panels, based on the assessor's recommendation. It would be for the assessor to decide how s/he would interview employees or people involved and, in the case of a diocese seeking recognition, how many parishes would need to be contacted.

Support structure

The implementation of Investors will be primarily at a diocesan level. It is clear that dioceses will need advice on the application of Investors, and that there is value in continuing dialogue at a national level with IIPUK. A group of people has been set up by the Board of Education to monitor progress, make recommendations, provide a pool of expertise, and liaise with IIPUK and others. One board officer would be designated to act as secretary to that group and to make available two days per month (on average) to co-ordinate work on Investors nationally, to field enquiries, to be a clearing house, to maintain Web pages and to facilitate other work. The specific work that the group would undertake would include the following.

TRAINING THE TRAINERS

One of the Technical Group members, Fred Ayres, has developed a course on the application of Investors in the Church for diocesan advisers and senior staff. This was successfully piloted with the Diocese of Bangor, and refined as a result. The course would be administered through the Board of Education Adult National Programme, and recruitment for it would be through all diocesan networks. The aim would be to introduce Investors to senior diocesan staff, would-be co-ordinators and those who might be key promoters in their dioceses.

COURSES FOR ADVISERS

Christians who are professionally qualified as Investors advisers and assessors are a major resource for the Church. The Technical Group of Investors experts has played a key role in the work of the Task Group. We have developed a course of theological reflection for advisers and assessors, to enable them to come to grips with the particularity of the Church and the biblical and theological issues involved in introducing Investors.

INTERNET

We propose that Internet pages be developed as part of the Church of England Web site. These pages would contain information about Investors, a summary of this book, training materials, contacts, references and email enquiries. We believe that this would be a low-cost and effective way of enabling best practice to be spread, and for expertise to be built up among parishes and dioceses engaging with Investors.

ADVICE FOR BISHOPS' COUNCILS

We have already received a number of requests from dioceses to share the experience we have gathered. Only so much can be done through the printed page. An important job for the group would be to offer advice and consultancy to the senior staff of dioceses and bishops' councils as they considered the application of Investors.

LIAISON WITH TECS

The network of 72 Training and Enterprise Councils would be important to every diocese engaging with Investors. They do not always understand the particularities of the Church and, unfortunately, their boundaries don't coincide with dioceses. The group would ensure that TECs were aware of the guidelines for Investors in the Church and were able to offer the most appropriate support.

The ecumenical dimension

There is a need to build on the initial work we have done through CCBI and CTE to share best practice across denominations. This work holds great promise for a mutual engagement with mission at a practical level.

6

Using Investors in the Church

Six steps to engage with Investors

- A considered decision, 'Is it for us?'
- A diagnostic exercise of where you currently stand.
- An action plan to enable you to work towards meeting the Standard.
- Implementation of the action plan over one to five or more years.
- Assessment and recognition.
- Continuous improvement.

These six steps have already been described in Chapter 1. Here we describe them as they would apply to a diocese of the Church. These are flexible guidelines, subject to local variation and adaptation.

1. Is it for us?

Open a discussion at Bishop's Council.

Look at other experiences of Investors: for example, those of church schools or experienced lay people. Make contact with the National Church Group to identify and learn from existing initiatives. Explore theological issues.

Explore how Investors could help the diocese.

Make recommendation to proceed with either Model A or Model B (see pages 67–8).

Progress to diagnostic exercise.

Feed back progress to Bishop's Council.

2. A diagnostic exercise

The diagnostic exercise is a means of establishing an answer to the question 'How do we already measure up?' It may be that the diocese has already established aims and a mission strategy. If that is the case, particular units in the diocese may be asked how they think they are meeting these aims, what implications have been raised for training, etc. Where aims and mission strategy are not already in place, the diocese may wish to undertake a SWOT analysis or more formal kind of audit. Use may be made of some of the key indicators from the Investors framework.

3. An action plan

At this stage the diocese will ask:

- What shall we work on, now and later?

- Who will do it (team of advisers)?

- Who will lead it (co-ordinator)?

- How will we evaluate?

- What resources will be needed?

TRAINING A PROJECT TEAM IN THE DIOCESE

The successful development of Investors in a diocese will require the selection and training of a co-ordinator and a project team of Investors advisers. In Investors jargon these are called 'Investors Champions', indicating that they have a promotional as well as advisory role. We do not feel this would be an acceptable term in the Church and prefer the term 'Adviser'. The co-ordinator and advisers need to have:

- knowledge of what is going on in the diocese and of its current needs and priorities;

- the trust and confidence of the senior staff and Bishop's Council;

- the trust and confidence of clergy and lay leaders as well as anyone employed by the diocese;

- knowledge of Investors;

- a working knowledge of training and development;

- some knowledge and experience of dealing with people, especially in a supervisory or managing capacity.

A two-day course was developed as a pilot training opportunity for Investors advisers in the Diocese of Bangor. It consisted of sessions on Investors and the various technical issues and questions involved in the process, and it gave an opportunity to probe seriously, 'Is this for us?' It was felt in evaluation that this was very important in exploring difficulties and in gaining confidence in understanding the Investors process. In Bangor, the bishop and senior staff were involved in the training, and this is recommended in other dioceses. For some clergy it was the first time they had been involved in joint training with their bishop and it was welcomed enthusiastically.

For those who might wish, there would be the possibility of using the course and further experience to acquire one of two formal qualifications: the 7436 Certificate 'Introducing Investors in People', awarded by the National Council for Further Education; and NVQ Level 4 Training and Development (part of the Human Resource Development NVQ), awarded by the Institute of Personnel and Development.

4. Implementation of the action plan

The action plan is put into effect and progress reported back regularly to the Bishop's Council. Important issues may be:

- What training is needed at particular stages?

- What external help is required, for example from the national group or the TEC?

- What links with others might be helpful?

5. Assessment and recognition

There are several kinds of information that the assessor will require in order to build up a picture of a diocese's life and work. Here are some examples of what a church in the diocese might provide towards this, and of what employee details should be given:

- History: materials that tell something of the story of the church and parish, what have been some of the key stages in its development, what are its current needs and how these have been assessed. This does not necessarily have to be in written form. It may be in collections of suitably annotated photographs; or perhaps some-one may already have produced a local history or made a video.

- Storyboards: these are descriptions of groups or activities in the life of the congregation. Again, lots of writing is not required. Pictures could be used, or post-its attached to a large picture on the wall. The task is to find imaginative ways of communicating the life of the church to someone who does not know it. Remember, the material could be used subsequently to introduce the church to other visitors or newcomers.

- *Organization chart*: a description of all the people who are involved in running or contributing to the life of the church – members of the PCC, readers, choir, servers, organist, sidespeople, intercessors, group leaders, carers, hall secretary, cleaner, etc. Again, it is better to use photographs. Many churches and cathedrals show their work in photographs and 'mug shots' of everyone involved.

- *Employee details*: information about those who are employed by the diocese or parish on a full- or part-time basis, and about those who are self-employed but working mainly for the diocese or parish. The details should include such things as name, job title, date of commencement of employment.

An important part of working towards recognition is the provision of evidence. There are three main approaches to this:

- PORTFOLIO. This is the traditional route and involves the organization collecting detailed evidence to demonstrate that it meets each of the requirements of the Standard. This could mean a considerable amount of work, finding copies of PCC minutes, getting statements of purpose and training objectives, and so on. In fact, only one *specially written* piece of information is required by the assessor: 'a written and flexible plan setting out the organization's goals and targets'. This does not have to be a lengthy document and could be an A2 flip chart at the back of a church or in the diocesan office. There must also be a plan which identifies training and development needs, but this can be shown by already existing material – for example, minuted PCC decisions or a notice advertising a forthcoming training event, and so forth. To avoid a large-scale 'paper exercise', the diocese can work with the adviser to identify where evidence is already to be found, rather than spending lots of time creating it. The task is 'how to share our story'.

- STORYBOARDS AND MATRIX. Another approach is to set out in large charts, rather like an organizational chart, the various ways in which the Standard is being met by the groups and sub-groups which make up the diocese's life. This can be straightforward or considerably complex, depending on your size!

- WORKBOOK. A more recent approach is the development of a workbook. This organizes the 23 indicators of the Standard into a central spine of five main areas, from which all the other processes emanate. It provides a simplified way of working step by step through setting out targets and evaluating how things are achieved, and avoids the need for masses of paperwork. The workbook approach would be especially helpful for parishes looking for internal review and the Bishop's Award (see pages 69–70) rather than external recognition.

6. Continuous improvement

The Investors process is a spiral of continuous review and evaluation. The real test of Investors is the ability of the organization to make the Standard endemic to its life. Until recently, organizations were re-assessed after three years. Now there is the option of the 12- to 15- month review and about 75 per cent of organizations are taking this. It is a shorter, non-portfolio process and focuses on specific aspects of the organization. It offers immediate feedback.

7

Conclusions

The Task Group is pleased to present this report to the Church. We have carefully examined Investors in People and its use by the Church and we have addressed a number of practical and theological questions and objections. We have been impressed with the confidence and sense of purpose which Investors has helped people to foster in parishes and dioceses. We have addressed issues to do with Investors as a management tool, together with many wider questions of management and change to which it gives rise. It is not a perfect model and it is not the only model. Much more work needs to be done on interpreting and simplifying the process for use by churches and we believe we have made a significant contribution to this. A detailed examination of other models in use by dioceses was beyond our brief and resources. We hope very much that the General Synod and the Archbishops' Council will continue to audit other models and approaches by the Church at different levels, and to disseminate learning and best practice.

The members of the Task Group and of the Technical Group who have advised us are confident that Investors can offer the Church at the present time an effective and theologically appropriate framework for development and training. Our reasons, set out in the foregoing discussion, can be summarized in the following points:

- There is a need in the Church for a coherent framework for development and training which would enable the different parts and levels of the Church to make a more fully integrated response to mission and ministry in the new millennium.

- Investors offers a people-focused way of meeting that need, and offers the Church a common language and approach. These are capable of recognizing the diversity between parishes and dioceses, yet offer a means of setting common goals in mission and of evaluating and learning from good practice.

- In making use of Investors, the Church would express a partnership with other institutions concerned with good practice and demonstrate its willingness both to learn and to contribute.

- Investors offers a means by which the Church could express its commitment to lifelong learning, develop as a learning organization and contribute to the development of 'a Learning Age'.

Appendix 1

Members of the Task Group

Mrs Lesley Wells, Member of General Synod and Board of Education (Chair)

Mr John Cridland, Director of Human Resources, Confederation of British Industry

The Revd Julian Cummins, Managing Director, AVISTA

Mr Nicholas Denison, Diocesan Secretary, Bath and Wells

The Revd David MacPherson, MSF Union

The Very Revd Peter Marshall, Dean of Worcester

Ms Catherine Mountford, Personnel Officer, Church Commissioners

Ms Angela Sarkis, Director, Church Urban Fund

The Revd Phil Williams, Vicar of Lenton Abbey, Nottingham

Staff

The Revd Ian Stubbs, Adviser in Adult Education and Lifelong Learning, Board of Education

Appendix 2

Members of the Technical Group

The Revd Julian Cummins, Managing Director, AVISTA (Chair)

Mr Fred Ayres, Director, Action Learning Ltd, IIP Adviser and Assessor

Mr Martin Bird, Senior Manager and Assessor, Birmingham and Solihull TEC.

Mr Don Jeffery, IIP National Assessor

Mr Richard Rose, Senior Assessor and Recognition Unit Manager, Birmingham and Solihull TEC.

The Revd Dr Graham Loveluck, Director of Education, Diocese of Bangor

Martin Smith, IIP Adviser, Surrey TEC

Mr Bob Thackwray, Professional Consultant, UCoSDA,

Mr Gary Matthews, Managing Director, Quality Services, Central London TEC

Mrs Lesley Wells, National Verifier NVQ, General Synod Member

Staff

The Revd Ian Stubbs, Adviser in Adult Education and Lifelong Learning, Board of Education

Appendix 3

A Glossary for the Church of England

Investors in People was developed in a business context, and its language reflects this. However, more than a third of organizations that have achieved the Standard are not businesses. They include schools, hospitals and charities. To a greater or lesser extent, all of them need to understand the language of Investors in a way that suits their ethos. To do so is not to subvert the Standard, but to understand the principles behind it in a deeper way. It enables organizations of many types to use a single Standard of a little over 400 words in a way that is both consistent and flexible. This is reflected in the guidance criteria offered by IIPUK on the interpretation of the Standard. The glossary here extends that interpretation for the Church of England.

Aims: what the organization is trying to achieve in broad terms. It is encapsulated in the diocesan statement of purpose.

Authorized ministry: people working for the delivery of the liturgical, evangelistic, educational and pastoral ministry of the Church, under the authority of the bishop, a board, synod or PCC, normally in a team.

Business objectives: the purpose of the diocese, as set out in the diocesan statement of purpose.

Employee: anyone who contributes to the achievement of the diocese's objectives. This means all members of synods and PCCs and all those engaged on an employed, self-employed or volunteer basis in authorized ministry or work under the authority of the bishop, a synod, board or PCC.

Employment: the period during which a person is a member of a synod or PCC or undertaking authorized ministry or work.

Evaluation: the process which identifies whether the activity has achieved its objectives, and which identifies the impact of the activity and informs further action.

Goals and targets: planned levels of performance for the diocese, teams and individuals, in relation to its statement of purpose. 'Goals' may be aspirational, whereas 'targets' should be specific, measurable, agreed, realistic and time-bound.

Investor in People: the diocese understood as an entity, as 'church'; in human terms, all those responsible at any level, as a manager, a person in authorized ministry, or a member of a synod or PCC, for what the diocese is and does.

Job-related: relevant to what each individual can contribute in particular authorized ministry or work or as a member of a synod, board or PCC.

Manager: any person with responsibility for leading or co-ordinating the ministry or work of others.

Objectives: the outcomes that are sought from a specified action or set of actions.

Organization: the diocese.

Recruitment: the point at which a person takes up membership of a synod, board or PCC or takes on authorized ministry or work.

Regular: happens at least annually, but may be more frequent.

Representative structures: PCCs, synods and boards.

Resources: people, time, gifts, facilities, expertise, equipment and money.

Team: a collection of individuals who come together to work towards a common goal or fulfil a common task. Examples include worship teams in parishes, teams of support ministers, specialist teams in areas such as social responsibility, teams set up for particular projects and formal teams such as PCCs.

The Top: the bishop in synod.

Top management: the bishop's staff.

Training and development: any activity that develops skills and/or knowledge and/or attitude and/or behaviour.

Vision: used interchangeably with 'Aims'.

Work: secretarial, administrative, executive or manual activities in support of the ministry of a church, under the authority of the bishop, a board, synod or PCC.

Appendix 4

The Investors in People Standard Applied to the Church of England

The unit referred to here is the diocese. What follows can be adapted to another unit such as a single parish or a cathedral.

THE INVESTORS STANDARD	APPLIED TO THE CHURCH

PRINCIPLE 1: COMMITMENT

An Investor in People makes a commitment from the top to develop all employees to achieve its business objectives.	**An Investor in People makes a diocesan commitment to develop all church people to carry out the church's mission and ministry.**
1.1 The commitment from top management to train and develop employees is communicated effectively throughout the organization.	1.1 There is a public commitment from the bishop in synod to develop people in community.
1.2 Employees at all levels are aware of the broad aims or vision of the organization.	1.2 Church members at all levels are aware of the broad aims and vision of the diocese.
1.3 The organization has considered what employees at all levels will contribute to the success of the organization, and has communicated this effectively to them.	1.3 The diocese has developed a common vision of how people at all levels will contribute to the church's mission and has shared this with them.
1.4 Where representative structures exist, management communicates with employee representatives a vision of where the organization is going and the contribution employees (and their representatives) will make to its success.	1.4 The diocese uses the synodical processes to ensure good two-way communication between itself and the parishes regarding the part that people can play in contributing to the church's mission and ministry at every level.

THE INVESTORS STANDARD   APPLIED TO THE CHURCH

PRINCIPLE 2: PLANNING

An Investor in People regularly reviews the training and development needs of all employees.

2.1 A written but flexible plan sets out the organization's goals and targets.

2.2 A written plan identifies the organization's training and development needs, and specifies what action will be taken to meet those needs.

2.3 Training and development needs are regularly reviewed against goals and targets at the organization, team and individual level.

2.4 A written plan identifies the resources that will be used to meet training and development needs.

2.5 Responsibility for developing people is clearly identified throughout the organization, starting at the top.

2.6 Objectives are set for training and development actions at the organization, team and individual level.

2.7 Where appropriate, training targets are linked to achieving external Standards, and particularly to National Vocational Qualifications (NVQs) and units.

An Investor in People regularly reviews the training and development needs of all church people.

2.1 A written but flexible plan sets out the diocese's agreed goals and targets.

2.2 A written plan identifies the diocese's training and development needs, and specifies what action will be taken to meet those needs.

2.3 Training and development needs are regularly reviewed against goals and targets at the diocesan, parish and individual level.

2.4 A written plan identifies the resources that will be used to meet training and development needs.

2.5 Responsibility for developing people is clearly identified throughout the diocese, starting at senior staff level.

2.6 Objectives are set for training and development actions at the diocesan, parish and individual level.

2.7 Where appropriate, training targets are linked to achieving external Standards, and particularly to National Vocational Qualifications and units.

THE INVESTORS STANDARD   **APPLIED TO THE CHURCH**

PRINCIPLE 3: ACTION

An Investor in People takes action to train and develop individuals on recruitment and throughout their employment.

An Investor in People takes action to train and develop individuals on baptism and throughout their lives.

3.1 All new employees are introduced effectively to the organization and all employees new to a job are given the training and development they need to do that job.

3.1 All baptized Christians are introduced effectively to the church and given the training and development they need to live a Christian life and exercise their discipleship and ministry.

3.2 Managers are effective in carrying out their responsibilities for training and developing employees.

3.2 Diocesan staff, clergy and lay leaders are effective in carrying out their responsibilities for training and developing church members.

3.3 Managers are actively involved in supporting employees to meet their training and development needs.

3.3 Diocesan staff, clergy and lay leaders are actively involved in supporting church members to meet their training and development needs.

3.4 All employees are made aware of the training and development opportunities available to them.

3.4 All church people are made aware of the training and development opportunities available to them.

3.5 All employees are encouraged to help identify and meet their job-related training and development needs.

3.5 All church people are encouraged to help identify and meet their training and development needs in relation to living a Christian life and fulfilling their dis-cipleship and ministry.

3.6 Action takes place to achieve the training and development needs of individuals, teams and the organization.

3.6 Action takes place to achieve the training and development needs of individuals and the church as a whole at every level.

THE INVESTORS STANDARD   **APPLIED TO THE CHURCH**

PRINCIPLE 4: EVALUATION

An Investor in People evaluates the investment in training and development to assess achievement and improve future effectiveness.

An Investor in People evaluates the investment in training and development to assess achievement and improve future effectiveness.

4.1 The organization evaluates the impact of training and development actions on knowledge, skills and attitude.

4.1 The diocese evaluates the impact of training and development actions on the development of gifts and competences.

4.2 The organization evaluates the impact of training and development actions on performance.

4.2 The diocese evaluates the impact of training and development actions on the development of the church's mission.

4.3 The organization evaluates the contribution of training and development to the achievement of its goals and targets.

4.3 The diocese evaluates the contribution of training and development to the achievement of its goals and targets.

4.4 Top management understand the broad costs and benefits of developing people.

4.4 Diocesan leaders understand the broad costs and benefits of developing people.

4.5 Action takes place to implement improvements to training and development identified as a result of evaluation.

4.5 Action takes place to implement improvements to training and development identified as a result of evaluation.

4.6 The management's continuing commitment to training and developing employees is demonstrated to all employees.

4.6 The diocese's continuing commitment to training and developing people is demonstrated to everyone.

Appendix 5

Strategic Review of the Investors in People Standard

Early in 1999 Investors in People UK started a strategic review of the Investors in People Standard. The following is part of the submission of the Task Group to the review process.

We very much welcome the opportunity to respond to this consultation paper. The Church of England is involved with Investors through projects in the dioceses of Ripon, Southwell, Bath and Wells and Lichfield, and through the many Church schools that are recognized as Investors in People. Together with our ecumenical partners we are closely involved with business through Industrial Mission in every part of the country. The role of business in the modern world is of practical and theological concern to Christians at work and has been the subject of frequent comment by the Archbishop of Canterbury and other Church leaders.

Our response to this consultation is based on our active participation in Investors and on this wider perspective. It includes engagement with those who suffer from aspects of modern management practice. We welcome the involvement of organizations representing a third of UK employees in Investors. We also welcome this review of the standard and its explicit endorsement of *The Learning Age*. For Investors to continue to thrive, we believe those responsible for the standard must listen to the voices of the managed as well as managers, and take seriously the experiences of those who have not always found the application of Investors to be beneficial.

We would like to make four overall points before addressing in turn each of the options you identify in the consultation paper.

Overall Points

1. We welcome the statement 'What we refer to the standard we mean the four principles (Commitment, Planning, Action and Evaluation) which are supported by the indicators and guidance'. This is how we have always understood Investors, but it is not always presented

that way at local level. TECs can sometimes put a narrow and pre-scriptive stress on the indicators, as if they are the standard rather than supportive of it. Many of the difficulties of application would be eased if this broad interpretation became universally adopted.

2.   We welcome the statement 'the standard should exist with the most appropriate format to meet customer needs'. Progress was made at the last review in making the standard more inclusive by replacing reference to 'business' with reference to 'organizations of every kind'. Its language should reflect this by being inclusive at every point.

3.   The paper helpfully refers at various points to public, private, voluntary and other organizations. It does not do so consistently, and sometimes the 'third sector' is omitted. No 'third sector' orga-nizations are listed among the 'strategic partners' that have already been consulted. Government has recognized the enormous role that churches voluntary organizations and community groups play in our society. We would be very happy to work with others to assist you in developing 'third sector' strategic partners.

4.   We believe the central value of Investors is the way the four principles set up a virtuous cycle of individual, team and organizational learning. It is an action learning model. It reflects the cycle of commitment, action and reflection that is at the heart of the practice of faith. As organizations operate this cycle, we believe they are drawn into a deeper understanding of their inter-dependence as people united by a common goal, who grow and learn together. Studies of the most successful business organization show that shared purpose and values are at their heart. Ethos and culture are increasingly seen to be crucial to the way organizations behave. We believe this reflects profound truths about the nature of human relationality, and about the potential for individual and collective fulfilment. Christians have been working with these issues for centuries. We believe that this perspective could be of real value in deepening the effectiveness of Investors. We would be very happy to work with you to develop this understanding.

References

Archbishops' Commission on the Organization of the Church of England (Turnbull Report), *Working As One Body*, Church House Publishing, 1995.

Board of Education, *Tomorrow is Another Country*, Church House Publishing, 1996.

Board of Mission, Mission Theological Advisory Group, *The Search for Faith and the Witness of the Church*, Church House Publishing, 1996.

Colin Buchanan, *Is the Church of England Biblical?: An Anglican ecclesiology*, Darton, Longman and Todd, 1998.

J. C. Collins and J. I. Porras, *Built to Last: Successful Habits of Visionary Companies*, HarperCollins, 1994.

R. Currie, A. Gilbert, L. Horsley, *Churches and Churchgoers*, CUP, 1977.

G. Davie, *Religion in Britain Since 1945*, Blackwell, 1994.

DfEE, *The Learning Age: A Renaissance for a New Britain*, 1998.

Ulrich Duchrow, *Global Economy: A confessional issue for the churches?*, WCC Publications, 1987.

John Finney, *The Well Church Book: A Practical Guide to Mission Audit*, CPAS, 1991.

David Ford, *Exposition of Scripture at the Eucharist (Ephesians 1.1-10)*, General Synod, 4 July 1998.

Kevin Giles, *What on Earth is the Church: An exploration in New Testament theology*, HarperCollins/Dove, 1995.

R. Gill, *Beyond Decline: A Challenge to the Churches*, SCM Press, 1988.

Robert K. Greenleaf, *Servant Leadership*, Paulist Press, 1991.

R. Greenwood, *Reclaiming the Church*, Fount, 1988.

C. Handy, *Understanding Voluntary Organizations*, Penguin, 1988.

J. Hillage and J. Moralee, *The Return on Investors*, Report 314, Institute of Employment Studies, 1996.

House of Bishops, *Eucharistic Presidency: A theological statement*, Church House Publishing, London, 1997.

John Kay, *Foundations of Corporate Success*, OUP, 1993.

C. Landry *et al.*, *What a Way to Run a Railroad – An Analysis of Radical Failure*, Comedia, 1985.

C. Landry *et al.*, 'An analysis of radical failure', in J. Batsleer, C. Cornforth and B. Paton, *Issues in Voluntary and Non-profit Management*, OU/Addison Wesley, 1992.

Paul Minear, *Images of the Church in the New Testament*, Lutterworth Press, 1961.

Christopher Moody, *Eccentric Ministry: Pastoral Care and Leadership in the Parish*, Darton, Longman and Todd, 1992.

Gareth Morgan, *Images of Organization*, Sage Publications, 1997.

Stephen Pattison, *The Faith of the Managers: When Management Becomes Religion*, Cassell, 1997.

Richard Roberts, 'An Executive Church?', *New Directions*, January 1996.

W. Schneider, 'Aligning strategy, culture and leadership', in J. Neumann, K. Kellner and A. Dawson-Shepherd (eds), *Developing Organizational Consultancy*, Routledge, 1997.

P. Senge, *The Fifth Discipline Fieldbook*, Nicholas Brealey, 1994.

Anthony Thiselton, *Interpreting God and the Postmodern Self: On Meaning, Manipulation and Promise*, T&T Clark, 1995.

R. Warren, *Building Missionary Congregations*, Church House Publishing, 1995.

R. Warren, *Signs of Life: How Goes the Decade of Evangelism?*, Church House Publishing, 1996.

R. Warren, Unpublished paper given at conference on 'The Church as a Learning Organization', 26 March 1998.

R. Williams, *Resources of Hope*, Verso, 1989.

Paul Yates, 'The social construction of priesthood', *Theology*, Vol. ci, No. 799, Jan/Feb 1998.

Index

unity and diversity 64–5
see also Investors in the Church
clergy
improving morale through investors 58
increasing workloads 51
survey on attitudes to Investors 42–3
see also ministerial provision
collaboration, development of 61
collaborative/shared ministry 52–3
commitment, and Investors Standard applied to the Church 83
communication, Bath and Wells diocese 21
continuous learning, Investors as a culture of 59

Davie, Grace 48
Decade of Evangelism 53
Denison, Nick 20, 21, 22
Development Plan, Bath and Wells diocese 21
diagnostic exercise, for engaging with Investors 8
dioceses
Bath and Wells 19–22, 30, 36
decisions on resources 60
and Investors in the Church 66–71
advice for bishops' councils 71
cathedrals 68
external assessment 69–70
Model A (A Diocesan Plan) 67–8, 68–9
Model B (Diocesan Approval) 68–9
reasons for diocese as 'building block' 66–7
support structure 70–71
and organizational issues 56–7
reviews of diocesan structure 65
staff as 'Investors' 62
value of Investors to 58

vision and planning initiatives 49, 50–51
see also Ripon Diocese
Duchrow, Ulrich 38

ecclesiology
divergence in 31
Trinitarian 32–4, 36
ecumenical dimension 71
education, and the Church 35
Edward King Institute 53
Emmaus courses 35
employee details, and Investor assessment 75
Eucharistic Presidency, House of Bishops on 32
evaluation
and Investors Standard applied to the Church 86
theological 30–46
evaluation xiii
external standards, and the Church 4

failure, handling of 40–42
faith, and belonging to the Church 48, 49
financial viability, concerns about 50
Finney, John 24
Ford, Professor David xiii, 35
fruits of the Spirit, and theological evaluation of Investors 36–7

General Synod 77
experiences and opinions of investors 11–12
and the learning Church 66
Giles, Kevin 45
Gill, Robin 48
global economic system 37–8
goal setting
Bath and Wells diocese 21